cape DON'T TELL town

The Mother City's (hush-hush) must-do list

contents

INTRODUCTION

Don't tell a soul, but a host of fascinating people are quietly indulging their passions in and for the Mother City while the average person goes about oblivious. While the hordes traipse around the malls and highways, a more informed bunch relishes the charm of discreet cafés and twisting byways. Not necessarily top secret, these hush-hush venues are simply spots that don't usually fill the mass-market brochures. They are discovered by those with a little more soul, for it takes a curious eye sometimes to see the old in a new way. So if you want to find an eatery that millions of others haven't discovered already, meet some of the city's quirkiest individuals or explore Cape Town's great attractions in a far more interesting way, we have a few suggestions. A whole list, in fact, that we promise will inspire, delight or intrigue you. (Please just don't tell the others.)

Sheryl & Sam.

AUTHORS & PHOTOGRAPHER

A born-and-bred Capetonian, **Sheryl Ozinsky** is the Manager of Cape Town Tourism but never takes a holiday, and – although a teetotaller – she passionately promotes the Cape Winelands. Many would agree that Sheryl, who is always ready to raise the city's profile, *is* Cape Town.

Sam Woulidge is a true local: she doesn't have a problem with Cape Town drivers, she swears in Afrikaans and she considers the South-Easter to be a mere breeze. The former editor of *Cape Review* and the founding editor of *Cape etc*, Sam is editor of the *Time Out Cape Town Visitors' Guide*.

Jurie Senekal has been photographing Cape Town's days and nights for five years, and is most at home when he is travelling, whether it is from Woodstock to Salt River or from McGregor to Agulhas.

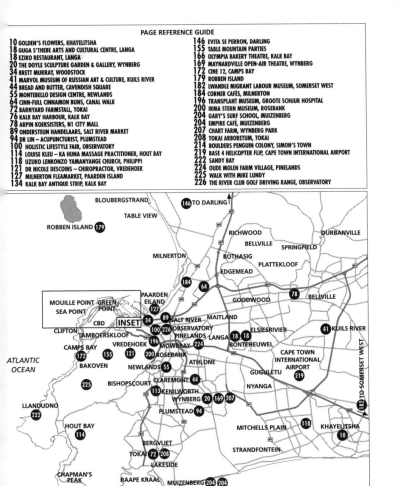

CAPE PENINSULA

MAP STUDIO 2003

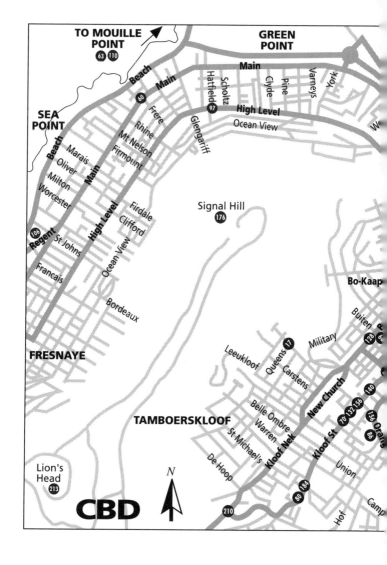

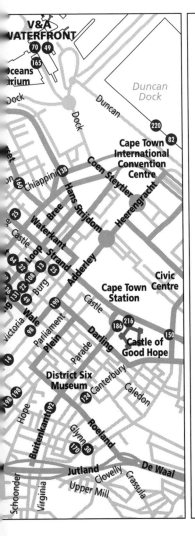

GUGA S'THEBE PG 18

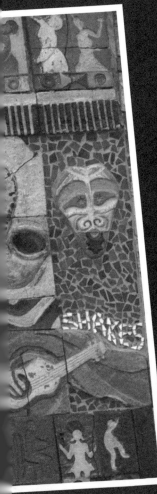

Art

CRAFT · FASHION · DESIGN

Creativity is rife in Cape Town. Stop at any traffic light and you will meet a crafter trying to sell beaded chameleons or outrageous pink plastic flamingos. For the people of Cape Town art is an integral part of life; you will see it on the hand-painted signs in an informal settlement as well as in the galleries where our celebrated artists exhibit. It is in the tin sunflower made in a shack as much as it is in the bronze sculpture that is shipped to Europe. Art depicts all that we fear, all that we love, all that we are.

flowers of faith

GOLDEN'S FLOWERS

Golden's flowers are legendary, not only for their artistic flair and innovative use of discarded material, but because the story of how they came to be is so inspirational. Each tin sunflower or rose serves as a reminder of everyday miracles.

A few years ago Golden Sonwabo Nonquase, disheartened and worried about how he was to support his family, had the first of three identical dreams. In these dreams, a voice told him to go to the rubbish dump, pick the flowers he would find there and sell them. After each of the first two dreams he went to the rubbish dump, but found nothing. Twice he returned home empty-handed and demoralised.

After the third dream, he again went in search of the promised flowers, but this time he noticed the brightly-coloured cooldrink tins on the dump. Still believing he had heard the voice of God, Golden took them home and made his first tin

daisy. Sunflowers and roses followed, then poppies and lilies.

Today Golden can create any type of flower from tin. Colourful flowers cover every available surface in his home and adjacent workshop – colourful testimony to this gentle soul's creativity and faith.

GOLDEN'S FLOWERS
Khayelitsha
By appointment only with a tour
Cape Town Tourism
021 426-4260

afro-chic

PAN AFRICAN MARKET

A stylish, original Art Nouveau entrance hall plays host to several large papier-mâché and wood-carved animals. It's the perfect backdrop for the myriad examples of African art on display within this building.

Here, over thirty stalls sell a vast variety of old and contemporary arts, crafts and artifacts. The range of fearsome African ceremonial masks is staggering, as is the quality of the beadwork. It is without a doubt Cape Town's best selection of African arts and crafts under one roof.

If the shopping proves too exhausting, put everything into your newly-acquired basket and head for the balcony of the Pan African Market Café, where you can overlook the activity on Long Street and contemplate the infinite possibilities of the African Renaissance!

PAN AFRICAN MARKET
76 Long Street, CBD
Mondays to Fridays, 9am till 5pm,
Saturdays, 9am till 3pm
021 426-4478

art attack!

SOUTH AFRICAN NATIONAL GALLERY

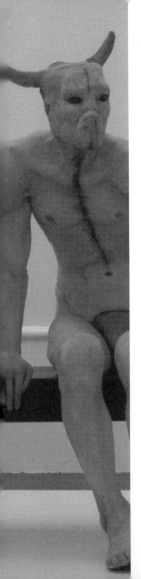

S ANG, as it is known, is a national treasure – with none of the stuffy connotations of a national gallery. In addition to the usual plethora of old masters, it is home to a comprehensive collection of contemporary South African art, and it is this that makes it such an incredible place.

Since the 1990s, under the leadership of the unstoppable and outspoken Marilyn Martin (now Director of Art Collections for the Iziko Museums of Cape Town), the National Gallery has embarked on an acquisition policy that 'acknowledges and celebrates the expressive cultures of the African continent, particularly its southern regions'. The result is intricate beadwork, woodcarvings and traditional craft alongside oil paintings, sculptures and video installations.

The gallery is truly representative of South African history, with an important collection of Resistance Art. The most

15

striking of these works is Jane Alexander's *The Butcher Boys*. This trio of malevolent figures with ripped open spines was sculpted in 1985 as a merciless commentary on the socio-political issues, terror and inhumanity of those times. These lifesize figures are a terrifying but fascinating presence in the gallery, and visitors are lured back to the piece time and again.

SANG is not a place to whizz through, or to visit only once. It is best explored at leisure and on weekday mornings when you will often find yourself alone in the large gallery spaces. Exhibitions are held regularly and often you can accompany exhibiting artists on a tour of their work.

IZIKO MUSEUMS OF CAPE TOWN
SOUTH AFRICAN NATIONAL GALLERY
Government Avenue, Gardens
Tuesdays to Sundays, 10am till 5pm
021 467-4660

creative clutter

PENNY DOBBIE GALLERY

Ever wandered through someone's home and liked something so much you wanted to buy it off them, there and then? Welcome to Penny Dobbie's world.

Penny's home is her gallery; the walls are full of wonderful works of art by South African artists and on every available surface stands an assortment of ceramics and sculptures. Her four well-fed, artistically-inclined cats laze amid the art, expecting as much, if not more, admiration.

Penny has run this gallery from her home for the past fifteen years and word of mouth keeps Capetonians knocking on her door. The work changes regularly and Penny, knowing exactly what her clients want, will inform them when appropriate pieces are for sale.

PENNY DOBBIE GALLERY
By appointment only
021 424-8349

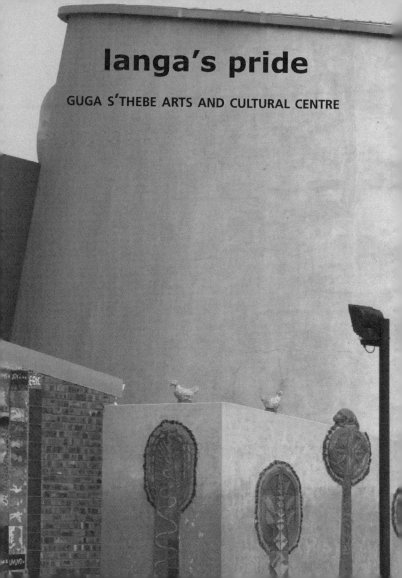

langa's pride

GUGA S'THEBE ARTS AND CULTURAL CENTRE

One of the most vibrant and creative buildings in Cape Town is to be found in Langa Township. The Guga s'Thebe Arts and Cultural Centre was designed by CS Studio Architects who worked with the community to come up with a design that is not only functional, but also fun.

The exterior and interior walls are covered with ceramics done by members of the public, and the place buzzes with energy. Laughter is heard during the drama classes, photographic exhibitions line the walls and music workshops are held regularly. The centre also houses the Zakheni (build yourself) beading project and visitors are welcomed.

While you're there, try the Eziko Restaurant. Also a cooking school, it has a menu that consists largely of traditional Xhosa fare – boerewors, pap and chakalaka, or samp and beans and home-made ginger beer.

GUGA S'THEBE ARTS AND CULTURAL CENTRE
Corner of Washington Avenue and Church Street, Langa
Mondays to Fridays, 10am till 5pm, Saturday mornings
021 695-3493 or 021 695-3328

EZIKO RESTAURANT
Corner of Washington Avenue and Jungle Walk, Langa
Mondays to Fridays, 10am till 4pm,
sometimes open on Saturdays
021 694-0434

fleshy bronze

THE DOYLE SCULPTURE GARDEN AND GALLERY

Jean Doyle's larger-than-life bronze sculptures are all gloriously unselfconscious women, boasting rotund bellies, exaggerated thighs and fleshy arms. They dance, they pose and they lounge. These are women who don't take themselves too seriously; women who unashamedly enjoy the good life.

Jean's studio and garden gallery in Wynberg is a fabulous celebration of flesh. Those who have admired her voluptuous sculptures might be somewhat surprised to meet an elegantly thin, soft-spoken artist. But, while Jean may not possess the ripe plumpness of her sculptures, she does have their sense of humour and innate sensuality. She also has a wonderful way of describing the characters who influence her work, and it is these words, as well as the work on display, that will leave you feeling inspired.

A visit means not only a wander around her garden filled with sculptures aged, coloured and polished by the elements, but also an opportunity to watch Jean at work.

THE DOYLE SCULPTURE GARDEN AND GALLERY
6 Mountain View Road, Wynberg
By appointment only
021 761-5081
www.doylebronzes.co.za

the visser landmark

PETER VISSER GALLERY

Peter Visser established his antique shop, specialising in maps and prints of Africa, more than thirty years ago. The Victorian building in which it is housed is almost as much of an attraction as the goods displayed within. It still stocks the maps and prints that it did all those years ago, but other unusual antiques can also be found here now.

The shop has evolved and is now one of the city's most impressive galleries, known for its wide array of ceramics and eclectic selection of antique and contemporary Africana.

The country's foremost ceramicists are represented here; Wendy McLachlan's *Terracotta pot with Winged Figure* once took pride of place, but the boldness of Barbara Jackson or Shirley Fintz have also attracted attention – as have Lindi Sales's picture boxes, which hang amid the religious icons and objets d'art.

23

The work changes frequently and visiting every so often to see what's on display and to chat to the charming and knowledgeable Peter Visser is a real pleasure.

PETER VISSER GALLERY
Corner of Long and Church streets, CBD
Mondays to Fridays,
8.30am till 5pm
Saturdays, 11.30am till 2pm
021 423-7870

monkeying around

MONKEYBIZ

Every now and then, you see something that makes you just so damn proud. Like Monkeybiz South Africa. In townships all over the Western Cape, women, under the guidance and leadership of Monkeybiz, are producing quality crafts that blend traditional beading skills with a modern edge. Craft becomes art, and tradition becomes trendy.

According to well-known ceramicists Barbara Jackson and Shirley Fintz, and Mataphelo Ngaka who started the project in 2000, Monkeybiz products cause a commotion wherever they are displayed. Shops in London and Tokyo are constantly re-ordering Monkeybiz dolls – the latest in Afro-chic. The beaded dolls and sculptures also recently caused a sensation at London's annual Sotheby's Contemporary Decorative Arts Exhibition where fifty pieces were snatched up by eager collectors. Orders were hurriedly placed because certain members of the aristocracy simply had to have a small beaded outhouse with figure sitting on a loo!

Monkeybiz South Africa is a non-profit organisation that's created employment for the most economically-disempowered members of our society while preserving an almost-forgotten craft. From their small beginnings, Monkeybiz now has more than 250 women making dolls, and almost as many on a waiting list to join the project.

On market days, you will encounter the artists with their babies on their back, proudly displaying their work. They laugh, share problems, compare designs and bargain over prices. They are economically empowered, have a sense of purpose and a creative satisfaction – for many this is a first.

The dolls are not your usual tourist buy; they are poignant images from these women's lives. Barbara Jackson is proudly ambitious: 'We want to be bigger than Barbie.'

MONKEYBIZ SOUTH AFRICA

There is an outlet at Cape Town Tourism,
Pinnacle Building, corner of Castle and Burg streets, CBD
Call to arrange a visit on market day and to
shop at 43 Rose Street, CBD
021 426-0145 or 021 426-5500
www.monkeybiz.co.za

a slick act

BELL-ROBERTS CONTEMPORARY ART GALLERY

This gallery/bookshop/café in the heart of the CBD is a great space for art lovers. What started off as a contemporary gallery and café is now also a publishing house specialising in art books. They produce beautiful coffee table books and art catalogues, as well as *Art South Africa*, an exciting quarterly print magazine on contemporary art – all of which can be bought in the gallery or browsed through in the café.

The artists represented here are some of the country's finest – Kevin Brand, Doreen Southwood, Brett Murray and Terry Kurgan – and it's wonderful to see their work exhibited in such a sophisticated space.

Brendan and Suzette Bell-Roberts aim to 'blast through the stalwarts of prejudices and cliques in establishing Cape Town as the capital of African art. And have a damn good time doing it all.' It appears they're doing just that.

BELL-ROBERTS CONTEMPORARY ART GALLERY
199 Loop Street, CBD
Mondays to Fridays, 8.30am till 5pm,
Saturdays, 11.30am till 1pm
021 422-1100
www.bell-roberts.com

designer fashion

MAYA PRASS

Maya Prass has an astounding reputation for someone who only launched her clothing label in 2000 and who is not yet on the wrong side of twenty-five. Magazines have picked up on her name – and her designs. She has been quoted as saying 'I offer an alternative to the mass-produced looks of the season. If commercial trends are the main road, I'm on the sidewalk.' Her studio is a riot of colour, and she emphasises colour, texture and pattern. Her clothes are confidently, boldly feminine: a rose print skirt is made from upholstery material and lined in bright yellow silk; another is made from braiding and saris. Maya is completely involved in every aspect of the design and manufacture of her clothes. 'My clothes are made with a lot of love,' she says fondly. 'Every piece that leaves here has a little piece of me inside of it.' She has deliberately held back on growing her business too much or too quickly. She only takes on as much as she can do herself, priding herself on the fact that each item is handmade. With overseas buyers making demands, Maya notes that her clothes have travelled more than she has. Not for long. This stylish girl is going places.

MAYA PRASS
021 465-5499 or 083 409-7051
Outlets include IndiaJane Designer Wear, Kalk Bay 021 7883020 and Claremont 021 683 7607; and from Purr Clothing, Kloof Street, Gardens, 021 424 5044

down the wire

STREETWIRES

Most traffic lights sport an artist or two selling their craft, be it a beaded chameleon, a star-shaped paper lantern or an intricate, true-to-the-original miniature Harley Davidson.

Here in Africa, necessity has given birth to astounding creativity. Streetwires has taken this one step further. In 2000 Patrick Schofield, Winston Rangwani and Anton Ressel started a social upliftment project with the intention of providing creative employment to as many wire-workers as possible. Their belief in the 'think global, act local' principle has spurred them on to worldwide success.

In the building on Shortmarket Street, wire-workers fulfil large orders of Christmas trees or wire radios (that really work!), or a range of corporate gifts. Some work on intricate commissions – such as the wire-art dress and tiara worn by one Ms Gay SA. If you're looking for a beaded ladybug, toys, heart-shaped key-rings, wine racks or even a magnificent wire chandelier, this is where you'll find it. You'll leave with a memory of a place that buzzes with creativity, where artists sing while they work and laughter is heard in all the rooms.

STREETWIRES
77 Shortmarket Street, CBD
Mondays to Fridays, 9am till 5pm
021 426-2475
www.streetwires.co.za

hitting the
funny bone

BRETT MURRAY

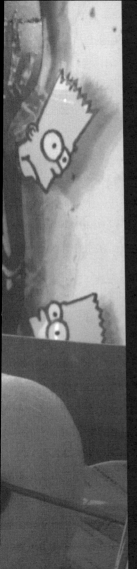

Some consider Brett Murray to be the bad boy of the South African art scene: talented and outspoken, he ignores polite society's insistence on political correctness. He has flawless political credentials and a Standard Bank Young Artist 2002 award. He is also responsible for the controversial statue in St George's Mall.

The three-metre-high bronze of an African curio, maniacally adorned with numerous bright yellow Bart Simpson heads, outraged many Capetonians and led to huge public debate. Murray was unrepentant: 'I like to make things that are provocative. *Africa* is a satirical piece; it's about living in South Africa and being exposed to a mixture of cultures.'

Brett Murray is brutally honest and he uses humour and art as his weapons of choice. He actively identified himself with the struggle for democracy and freedom in the 1980s and early 1990s and his work speaks of his convictions.

He used easily recognisable pop icons and altered them to convey both the tragedy and comedy of the South African psyche. Ritchie Rich became a black *Rich Boy*, depicting the changing face of capitalism. A triplicate of Bart Simpson-like faces with Afros shouted 'Ow' in *Change Is Pain*.

More recently he has turned his attention to the problems within our present ruling party. In an exhibition entitled 'White Like Me', Brett confronts xenophobia, censorship and what he sees as the new black fascism. The work consists of flat metal and plastic wall sculptures of single frame cartoons with unexpected dialogues. In *Zulu Heaven*, St Peter stands at the Pearly Gates and challenges a white man in a pin-stripe suit: 'Say... I want to go to heaven... in Zulu.' In another sculpture of four boys in party hats, one relays a message he has just received over the phone: 'It's the president... he says we must play dumb... sounds familiar.'

Brett Murray and his assistant, Shadrack Vara, work in a studio in Woodstock surrounded by blowtorch flames, wacky light-fittings, metal mantras proclaiming 'I must learn to speak Xhosa', and works in progress.

He also collaborates artistically with his friend Conrad Botes from Bitterkomix. Together they make a series, 'Boogie Lights', that features, among others, a tiny figure falling off (or jumping off?) the top of the Voortrekker Monument.

But what about political correctness? I ask.

Brett smiles. 'I wiped my ass with the white flag of fascism and I'll wipe it with the black flag of fascism. D'you know what I mean? And if I piss people off, so what? The Struggle will continue.'

BRETT MURRAY
Woodstock
By appointment only
021 447-1971

See his collaboration with San artist Stefaans Samcuia in the reception area of the Cape Town International Convention Centre

art rage

WILLIE BESTER

Willie Bester's art shows us the other side of Cape Town, the sadder side: its poverty and despair. His paintings are studies of marginalised communities and their daily existence. The work is powerful, all the more so because his subjects are treated with dignity – there is hope in a pair of scuffed red shoes, or a portrait of hands working at a small Primus stove.

Not only one of South Africa's foremost contemporary artists, Willie is also recognised as having played an important role in the Struggle years. His mixed media township scenes had a profound effect on those who saw them depicting the cruelties and inequalities of the ruling regime, while his commemorative portraits of Struggle leaders are a tribute to their courage and dedication.

Willie Bester couldn't be silenced in the 1980s and he won't be silenced now. His recent works are concerned with the issues and challenges facing the present government and once again Willie Bester's art is changing people's perceptions. His collages and salvage sculptures are critical of present injustices. Life-size sculptures, made from bits of scrap metal welded together, explore human rights abuses, such as those faced by Sara Baartman in the 1800s and the immigrants who were savagely attacked by police dogs more recently.

Smaller works depict life in urban informal settlements, where he focuses on ordinary people and their daily struggle.

Willie believes passionately in righting injustices and that changing people's perceptions through art is one way of achieving this. It pains Willie Bester, a soft-spoken, gentle man, to work continually with the darker side of humanity as his subject, but, as he puts it, 'There is no form of escape. Remaining apolitical is a luxury that South Africans simply cannot afford.'

WILLIE BESTER

Atlantic Art Gallery
41 Church Street, CBD
Mondays to Fridays, 10am till 4.30pm,
Saturdays, 10am till 1pm
021 423-5775

Association for Visual Arts
Metropolitan Gallery
35 Church Street, CBD
Mondays to Fridays, 10am till 5pm,
Saturdays, 10am till 1pm
021 424-7436

Rose Korber Art Consultants
By appointment only
021 438-9152

cape glasnost

MARVOL MUSEUM OF RUSSIAN ART & CULTURE

Those who grew up in the old South Africa will remember the *'Rooi Gevaar'* – and how anything Russian was regarded with distrust and venom. But now we are children of the universe and embrace all cultures.

Which is a very good thing because it has opened the way for a small museum in an old Cape Dutch manor house, where you'll find modern Russian paintings, religious icons and fabulous Fabergé eggs. In 1994 Dr Mark Veloshin bought one of the Cape's oldest wine farms and established the Marvol Museum of Russian Art and Culture on it.

When you've had your fill of Russian art, you can taste South African wines and lunch in the garden. The kids, having been dragged along, will be most impressed with the large duck pond and its fearsome geese.

MARVOL MUSEUM OF RUSSIAN ART & CULTURE
Hazendal Wine Estate, Bottelary Road (M23), Kuils River
Tuesdays to Fridays,10am till 4pm,
Saturdays and Sundays, 10am till 3pm
021 903-5112 or 021 903-5034

fashionable art

MEMEME

Modish Long Street has a myriad boutiques selling independent labels and sexy street fashion. Of these, Mememe is a stunning showcase for innovative young Cape Town fashion designers.

Conceptual artist Doreen Southwood and designer Kirsty Bannerman (of the Coppelia label) co-own this wonderful emporium that stocks an array of cutting-edge designers such as Richard de Jager, David West and Seth Harper, as well as their own designs. When last visited they were also stocking original jewellery by the creative and daring jewellery designer Carine Terreblanche.

Mememe is a delirious combination of art and fashion – a white polka-dot security gate and bright green faux grass doormat welcome you inside, while a pink metal poodle guards the cash register. The shop windows are display cabinets where designer clothes flaunt it alongside works by contemporary artists.

If you're looking for something original to wear, chances are you'll find it here, but, even if you're not that trendy or daring, you still need to have a look around.

MEMEME
279 Long Street, CBD
Mondays to Saturdays, 10.30am till 5pm
021 424-0001

art staples

BREAD AND BUTTER

The philosophy at Bread and Butter is that we need basic things to survive... but we need beautiful things to survive happily.

This original store is the product of the union between two creative minds: those of Paul Simon of Young Designers Emporium and artist and curator Kim Stern. Their belief in the need to merge commerce and art has led them to provide a space where artists and designers can sell their work – their proverbial bread and butter.

Bread and Butter does not house art, but rather special, freshly-inspired products conceptualised by well-known artists, each of whom has developed a product label unique to the store.

Which makes this the ultimate gift store where 'must have' becomes 'can have' because it's all an affordable, slick interpretation of the 'local is lekker' adage.

BREAD AND BUTTER
Shop F56A, Cavendish Square
Mondays to Saturdays, 9am till 5pm,
Sundays, 9am till 2pm
021 671-4204

capturing
the stillness

JOHN KRAMER

Aclosed café in the afternoon sun. A bicycle leaning against the stoep of the general dealer's store in a forgotten corner of the Karoo. There are no people in John Kramer's paintings, yet each is a portrait that conveys the history and personality of a place.

John Kramer's paintings portray ordinariness. Old buildings, peeling paint and faded advertisements embody the spirit of communities and times that have almost been erased. For John, buildings must have a feeling – something that has little to do with their architecture. It is how the viewer relates to a building that gives it significance. Those who respond to his work do so because something in it sparks recognition. It may be a colour, the store-front stoep, a Joko Tea plaque or a canvas awning, but it will remind someone of their past.

John's paintings symbolise four o'clock on Sunday afternoons. You can almost hear the call of the cicadas and smell the small town dust. For many, John's works are a poignant reminder of a childhood spent in small towns.

'I certainly understand or can relate to the scenes I paint,' John says. 'I can recall those quiet, boring Sunday afternoons... I've sat under verandas in small towns as a child, wishing that something exciting would happen. I remember those moods well. And I remember hating it. Looking back, it's one of the strongest recollections of childhood in a small town, and now one recalls those times with deep affection.'

JOHN KRAMER
Atlantic Art Gallery
41 Church Street, CBD
Mondays to Fridays, 10am till 4.30pm,
Saturdays, 10am till 1pm
021 423-5775

Penny Dobbie Gallery
By appointment only
021 424-8349

Rose Korber Art Consultants
By appointment only
021 438-9152

afro-quirk

AFRICAN IMAGE

If you are inspired by our continent, but are looking for something a little out of the ordinary in terms of African artifacts, find your way to this shop. African Image offers you the quirkier end of the African curio market.

Here you'll find those African creations that make your toes curl with sheer pleasure. Among the bright purple plastic chickens, tiny tin briefcases and lunch-boxes made from well-known brands' metal rejects, Madiba snow domes and carpets made from recycled Sunrise Toffee and Chappie wrappers, you'll also find those wonderful Warhol-inspired fabrics from the Philani Print Project and Monkeybiz dolls. They also stock a lovely selection of Ethiopian Coptic Crosses.

AFRICAN IMAGE
Corner of Church and Burg streets, CBD
Mondays to Fridays, 9am till 5pm,
Saturdays, 9am till 1.30pm
021 423-8385

Shop 6228, V&A Waterfront
021 419-0382

49

art admiration

ATLANTIC ART GALLERY

Riva Cohen is an integral part of the Cape Town art scene, the woman who has helped launch many careers and collections.

She carries an enormous amount of work by a wide variety of artists – the Slingsby's, Philip Badenhorst, Gail Caitlin, Hannetjie de Clerq, Mark Midgley, Willie Bester and John Kramer among others. Her gallery is crowded – to the point that she has run out of space and piles of valuable art rest against the walls, waiting for someone to find them.

Knowledgeable and passionate about art, Riva will make you feel right at home. All she asks is that when you leave you point to at least one work you love: here you don't need to buy, you only need to share her passion.

ATLANTIC ART GALLERY
41 Church Street, CBD
Mondays to Fridays, 10am till 4.30pm,
Saturdays, 10am till 1pm
021 423-5775

smart arts

ASSOCIATION FOR VISUAL ARTS

If your social life is lagging and your creative inspiration at an all-time low, get your name onto the mailing list of the AVA.

This contemporary art gallery, headed up by the dynamic Estelle Jacobs, is the one place in Cape Town with the power to draw laid-back Capetonians out of their nest on weekday evenings, come rain or shine.

Here, at gallery openings, everyone mills about, drinking wine and talking art and generally having a good time. It's because art at the AVA is accessible, interesting and generally a whole lot of fun.

AVA is a non-profit, membership-based arts association whose primary aim is the advancement of art and artists. In addition to its three-weekly exhibitions featuring both established and emergent artists, AVA runs an active Artreach programme for disadvantaged art communities.

53

The AVA's elected committee ensures vibrant works. This is the place to frequent if you're looking to acquire affordable pieces from some of South Africa's finest artists, and stay in the know vis-à-vis the Cape Town art scene.

Should you encounter Estelle in the gallery space, she will fill you in on the latest art happenings, offering insights and witty observations all the while. She's passionate about art; she'll affectionately stroke Sanell Aggenbach's herd of life-size black sheep while recounting the success of Willie Bester's recent exhibition, discussing Kevin Brand's sculptures or talking about a particularly difficult abstract piece of work. Estelle is an art addict – and she's more than willing to share her drug of choice!

ASSOCIATION FOR VISUAL ARTS
Metropolitan Gallery, 35 Church Street, CBD
Mondays to Fridays, 10am till 5pm,
Saturdays, 10am till 1pm
021 424-7436
www.ava.co.za

conservation
by design

MONTEBELLO DESIGN CENTRE

Montebello in leafy Newlands is exactly the sort of place to go to when one of you wants to commune with nature, while the other simply has to shop!

Cecil Michaelis, who owned the historic site and Montebello farm buildings, made the Design Centre possible with a financial and property bequest. It now houses a project that promotes good local design and craft as a means of job creation.

Set in a lush forest-like environment, despite being just off Newlands Avenue, the Centre has a wonderful sense of community: artists visit one another's studios, while visitors can watch creative people hard at work in really special surroundings.

You will marvel at organic metal sculptures dangling from the trees outside an industrial design studio, and be tempted to take home garden furniture and fencing made entirely of Port Jackson – an alien plant depleting our water resources. If you follow the fire, you will come across The Forge where blacksmith Nicolas Lehmann practises the 'art in ironmongery'. Examples of his work can also be seen on the gate of Sitali Jewellers where, in a fabulously converted Victorian stable (stalls intact!), you can talk to the jewellery designers who are producing seriously exciting stuff.

There is a nursery offering landscape design (aptly called The Greenhouse & Effects), as well as a popular restaurant, The Gardener's Cottage. Should you be in that 'I'm-looking-for-a-creative-outlet' headspace, you'll also find plenty of classes on offer, ranging from ceramics, printmaking and weaving to African music and dance.

MONTEBELLO DESIGN CENTRE
31 Newlands Avenue, Newlands
Mondays to Fridays, 9am till 4.45pm (but The Gardener's Cottage is closed on a Monday), Saturdays and Sundays, 9.30am till 2.30pm
021 685-6445

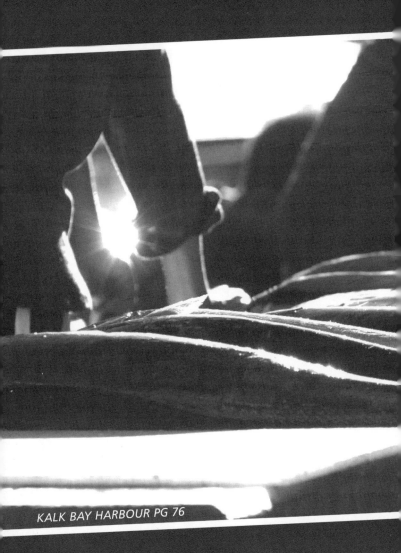

KALK BAY HARBOUR PG 76

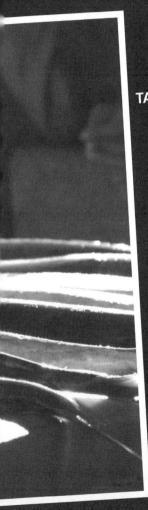

Food

TASTE · ATMOSPHERE · PRODUCE

The city's culinary secrets lie not in its myriad fine dining establishments, wonderful though they may be, but in its small neighbourhood eateries, street cafés and traditional home cooking. The spiciness of a samoosa, the syrupy sweetness of a koeksister, the sharp tang of sour-fig preserve, the comfort of warm farm bread and butter and fresh snoek will touch something deep inside you. Meanwhile the acquired taste of a good espresso, sashimi or tabbouleh will remind you that this is a city embracing many cultures.

a corner of lebanon

THE CEDAR RESTAURANT AND TAKEAWAY

Here's the secret: a girl and her love are not doomed to a lifetime of franchise burgers and pizza should the aforementioned girl (or her love) have neither the talent, nor the inclination, to rustle up dinners à deux. The Cedar is your solution to burnt pots and boredom.

A variety of wonderful Lebanese dishes can be ordered from this heartwarming family-run restaurant. Choose from freshly-made tabbouleh, stuffed eggplant, tahini, or cabbage leaves filled with tender cubes of lamb. You can even drop off your own pots and dishes should you wish to carry the pretense further and impress dinner guests.

David Davids is a Lebanese who came to South Africa thirty-two years ago and swept local girl Marlene off her feet. Today, together with their son Nigel, they make an awful lot of people happy at their unpretentious café. The Davids opened their small restaurant about three years ago. Business was quiet until a local, named Herman, visited and started telling people about this refreshingly unfashionable place. Word spread and soon it became the haunt of world-weary media types and locals looking for The Real Thing.

There are four small tables at The Cedar and those wishing to eat in are advised to call beforehand. Here, slightly squashed between the kitchen and the takeaway counter, eating wonderful food, you'll almost forget that you're not in an exotic location far away from slightly-seedy Sea Point Main Road.

When the evening rush is over, David will smoke the hargeleh while their daughter Beverley may or may not feel like belly-dancing. Sometimes, if the mood is right, her father and brother join her. Marlene will look on. You will sip strong Lebanese coffee and feel at home.

THE CEDAR RESTAURANT AND TAKEAWAY
76a Main Road, Sea Point
Mondays to Saturdays, 10.30am till late
021 433-2546

mouille point musts

NEWPORT MARKET AND DELI

If, as most Capetonians believe, life's too short to be wasted on bad wine, it's also just long enough to include wholesome meals with the best sea views!

Newport is where you'll be drinking a Mango Madness smoothie after a morning run on the Promenade, while the lazier among us gather for cappuccino and chocolate brownies before picking up a ready-made dinner.

For the owner, Cape Town icon Allan Schapiro, the kitchen is a place where the word 'fry' is forbidden, so there are no greasy breakfasts to be found at Newport.

And the cakes? Well, the decadent baked cheesecake and fabulous carrot cake can quite honestly be classified as a protein *and* a vegetable!

NEWPORT MARKET AND DELI
47 Beach Road, Mouille Point
Mondays to Sundays, 8am till 7pm
021 439-1538

sinfully sweet

CINN-FULL CINNAMON BUNS

I ronically enough, Bible House on Greenmarket Square is where you'll find the second branch of Cinn-full. This decadent café provides sustenance and sweetness to urban dwellers and workers. Think creamy café lattes and large cinnamon buns, drenched in a warm icing-sugar topping.

Sanelle le Roux's small blue and white café in Canal Walk is where it all started. Her offerings gave that Super-Sized-Extra-Large Shopping Mall some soul, while a cinnabun sugar rush gave tired shoppers the energy to continue their retail therapy. Thus Sanelle is single-handedly responsible for the cinnamon addiction that afflicts all who have tasted these mouth-watering marvels. While her offerings may be considered sinful, there are those who believe she's a saint.

CINN-FULL CINNAMON BUNS
Bible House, 38 Shortmarket Street, Greenmarket Square, CBD
Mondays to Fridays, 7am till 5pm,
Saturdays, 7am till 2pm
021 424-5249

Shop 187, Entrance 3, the lower level of Canal Walk
Mondays to Saturdays, 8am till 9pm,
Sundays 9am till 9pm
021 552-0026

salute amigo!

MEXICASA

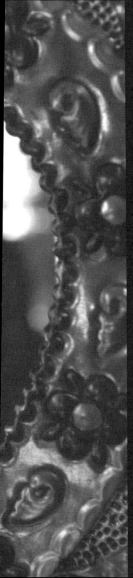

Like chillis, all things Mexican are red-hot in the fashion stakes. But authenticity is everything and there is a vast difference between Tex-Mex and Mexico City. MexiCasa offers you the opportunity of experiencing a real Mexican home without having to get your passport in order.

MexiCasa is the realisation of a dream shared by Capetonian Sandy Morland and her Mexican husband, Zeus Mancera Fuentes; they met and fell in love in Mexico and with their move to Cape Town they dreamt of creating a cultural exchange between Mexico and South Africa. The result is a small corner of Mexico in the heart of the Bo-Kaap – the suburb providing a suprisingly authentic backdrop to their dream.

Here, where two glittery skeletons guard the front door, their bright orange home doubles as a restaurant and an art gallery for wonderfully original pieces by some of Mexico's best-known artists and craftsmen. It's even a private party venue; book in advance and Sandy and Zeus will welcome your group of friends (anywhere between six and twelve people) and cook up a storm.

The recipes come from Zeus's family and Sandy's travels. She recounts tales of beach huts and simple foods, of mining towns and potent spices. Their passion for Mexico is infectious and inevitably you will take in more than just food in the course of your evening; you will learn about a different culture, about celebrating The Day of the Dead, of the poetry of pomegranates, that good tequila should only ever be sipped, and of the joy of breaking open a beautiful piñata.

MEXICASA
36 Buiten Street, Bo-Kaap
By appointment only
021 423-1202
www.mexicasa.co.za

sushi

MINATO

I f your style runs to conveyor belt sushi and designer décor, stay away. Minato is where taste is something applied to the food and not necessarily to the interior design. It is, nonetheless, housed in one of Cape Town's more interesting buildings – one decorated by artist Beezy Bailey and Koos Malgas of Owl House fame.

A glittery boot-clad, sunglass-wearing centipede welcomes you into the restaurant where you are instructed to 'order only once' to avoid confusion and irritation. No one adheres to this rule, so go wild with a superb election of sushi, sashimi and tempura and a good assortment of oriental beers. The food here is really good and surprisingly reasonable – which makes for a nice change from the more fashionable sushi restaurants in town.

MINATO
4 Buiten Street, CBD
Mondays to Saturdays, 6.30pm till late. Booking essential
021 423-4712

the caffeine scene

VIDA E CAFFE

Presiding over the sexiest café in town, owners Rui Esteves and Brad Armitage provide their clientele with all of life's essentials. Here you'll find great coffee, gorgeous muffins, freshly-squeezed orange juice, a stylish interior and the most fabulous loo in all of café society (think stainless steel, red lacquer and a reflective ceiling).

Orders are placed at the counter and your number is called out when your coffee is ready. The original branch is the one on Kloof Street, and it will always be the favourite among models and swish designer types. If you don't fall into these categories you're still most welcome – here, we're all treated the same. And should you have been told 'Sai daqui! Nos não temos cha!' and are wondering what that's all about, it means 'Get out! We do not have tea!'

VIDA E CAFFE
Shop 1, Mooikloof, 34 Kloof Street, Gardens
Mondays to Saturdays, 7.30am till 5pm
021 426-0627
www.caffe.co.za

Shop 6100
V&A Waterfront
8am till 9pm
021 425-9440

bella the pig

BARNYARD FARMSTALL

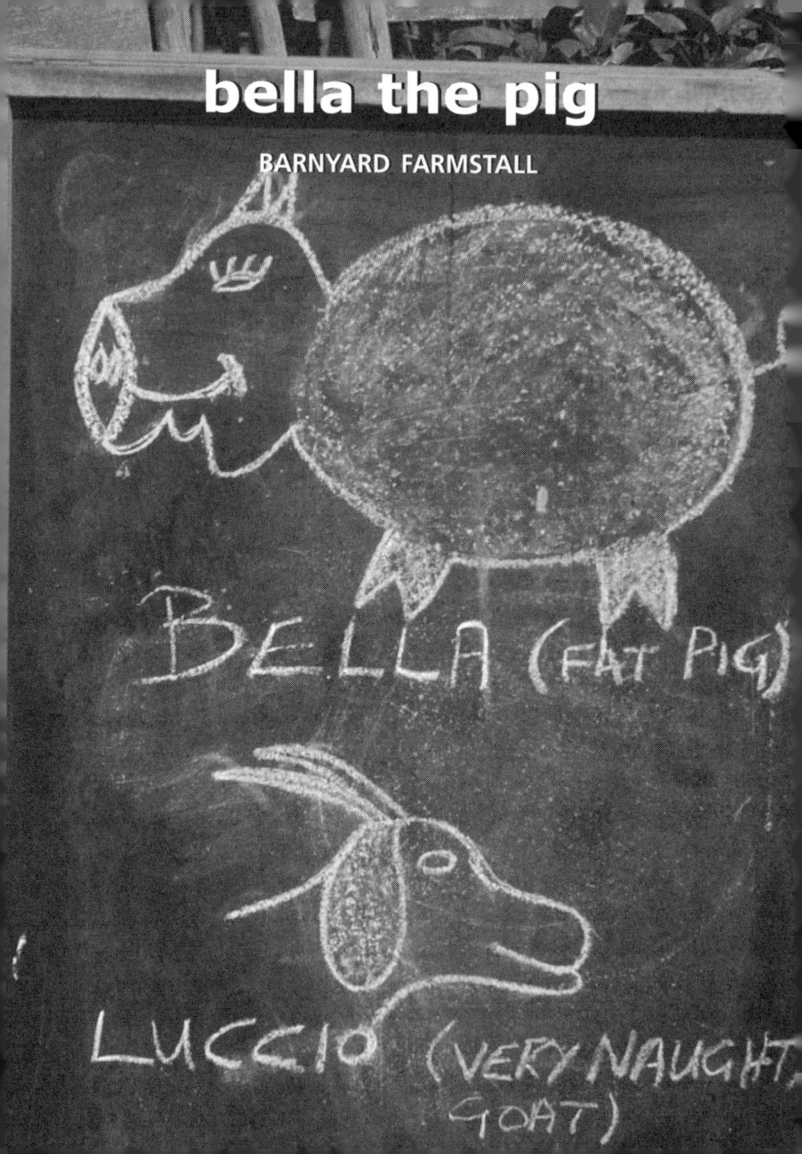

She's fat. She's beautiful. Her name is Bella and she's a pig. Literally! She's also the main attraction at the Barnyard Farmstall – and that takes some doing, because the competition is tough. Luccio, the very naughty goat, has his loyal followers while the many chickens are an endless source of amusement to some of the younger patrons. The playground/farmyard is also a great attraction and could divert attention.

Bella also has to compete with some of the best farm fare in the metropole. Thick slices of wholewheat bread served with farm butter and smoked snoek pâté will tempt you, as will the homemade cakes. And the traditional breakfasts, cooked on an old-fashioned coal stove, will appeal to the deep-rooted farmer's instinct in even the most hardened urbanite.

The shop sells old-fashioned ginger beer, homemade meals, raw honey on tap and free-range eggs, newly laid by the feathered folk who scratch around the lavender-fringed tea garden. An added bonus? The staff are great and really kid-friendly – hell, they even like grown-ups!

Barnyard Farmstall is a good stop before or after a visit to the nearby Steenberg wine estate. (Try to get your hands on a bottle of their Sauvignon Blanc Reserve 2001!)

One last thing: it's not a pleasant thought, but, should you visit the Barnyard and not find Bella, please don't order the bacon.

BARNYARD FARMSTALL
Steenberg Road, Tokai (at the bottom of Ou Kaapseweg between Steenberg Estate and the end of the M3)
Mondays to Sundays, 9am till 5pm
021 712-6934

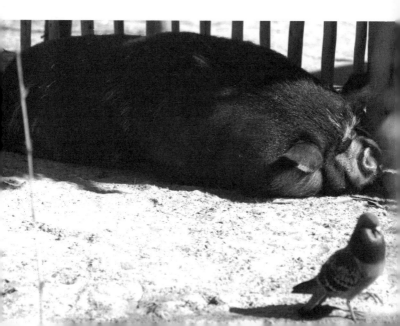

sensational samoosas

MOUNTAIN VIEW CAFÉ AND TAKEAWAYS

This is where you'll find some of the best samoosas in the city. Fried triangular pastries stuffed with spiced vegetables or meat, samoosas are the splendid offerings of Cape Malay cuisine, and no self-respecting café would be without them. Certainly, no celebration in the Cape would be complete if these weren't on the table.

The Mountain View Café also offers a good selection of other local specialities like curry and rice and traditional milk tarts that you can take away and try to pass off as your own!

MOUNTAIN VIEW CAFÉ AND TAKEAWAYS
219 Long Street, CBD
Mondays to Saturdays, 7.15am till 5.15pm
021 423-1852

fishy business

KALK BAY HARBOUR

This lively, working harbour is where you can buy the freshest fish – straight from the fishermen who went out at 2am to earn their living. You can watch the brightly-coloured wooden boats come in, and talk to the fishermen at the quayside. And, for a small fee, you can have your catch of the day scaled and gutted while you wait.

Should you prefer your fish cooked, Kalky's has the best takeaways. This unpretentious establishment has been serving the locals their fish and chips for years, and, if it's good enough for them, you can be sure it's good. At the harbour, you'll also find a vibrant sense of community; you'll hear raised voices and laughter and plenty of Cape lore and stories should you take the time to listen.

KALK BAY HARBOUR
Every day of the week, morning, noon or night, depending on when the fish are running

N1 koeksister man

ARPIN KOEKSISTERS

Most Capetonians will tell you: 'The best koeksisters come from the N1 Koeksister Man.' A koeksister, for those not yet in the know, is a doughnut, plaited, fried and dipped in syrup. They're delicious served cold, and are as South African as beer and biltong.

Eleven years ago Arno Arpin and his wife Hannelie started baking these traditional treats and selling them door-to-door. It proved such a successful venture that they gave up their day jobs and provided koeksister addicts around the northern suburbs with their daily fix from an informal trading spot near the N1 City Mall traffic lights. But this got up the nose of some Tygerberg officials and, after several court appearances, Arno and his koeksisters have relocated to a spot in the N1 City Mall, where a bag of eight syrupy knots still sells for R10.

Arpin is often a last stop en route to Cape Town International Airport; many a homesick South African abroad makes sure visiting friends bring a supply of the N1 Koeksister Man's finest with them.

ARPIN KOEKSISTERS

Entrance 1 of N1 City Mall. Head towards the flower sellers –
you will find Arno's koeksister cart near N1 Liquors
Mondays to Saturdays, 9am till 5pm
021 592-1819

fun food

DOUBLE "O" AND PAAPER BITES

You're unlikely to find these snacks and cooldrinks in other parts of the country. They are uniquely Cape phenomena.

Garishly-coloured Double "O" is sweet and satisfying – the perfect accompaniment to the savoury taste of Paaper Bites: bits of samoosa pastry infused with a variety of flavours. Both can be found at corner cafés and street vendors, and a huge part of their charm is the fact that when you chance upon them you're in the sort of place that typifies our Cape culture.

DOUBLE "O" AND PAAPER BITES

Corner cafés around the Peninsula – try Mr Bawa's on Kloof Street in Gardens, Rose's Corner Café in Rose Street, Bo-Kaap, and street vendors

81

the fortune cookie

JEWEL TAVERN

It's not all nautical chic down at the docks – there are still some authentic places. The kind of places where appetites for good food after a hard day's work – or a month at sea – are well satisfied.

For the many Taiwanese fishermen who dock at our shores, as well as landlubbers with a craving for real Chinese food, the Jewel Tavern offers just that. A once-humble little eatery, it has been spruced up, but it remains loyal to the principle of good food.

The sizzling beef is superb, or try the pork with chilli or chicken with cashew nuts. And the spring rolls more than pass the taste test.

JEWEL TAVERN
Off Vanguard Drive, Duncan Dock,
Cape Town Harbour
Mondays to Sundays,
mid-morning till 10pm
021 448-1977

wine-oh!

THE NOSE WINE BAR

Great! Someone's taken the *schlepp* out of being a wine snob. Frequenting The Nose is a bit like reading study guides on the classics and then confidently participating in a literary discussion. It's also heaven for those of us who have a hellish time making decisions.

The concept is simple and brilliant: a fabulously chic wine bar, specialising in South African wines, where you can buy over twenty different wines by the glass.

And the food is sublime – a fusion of Mediterranean and Asian flavours, cleverly offered in Peckish or Ravenous portions so that you can order a variety to accompany your choice of wines.

It's the sort of place you'll keep going back to, not least because of the laid-back attitude here. The Cape Quarter is also a great place to suss out what's happening on the design front with shops like East of Eden and Cigar. So after some inspirational browsing, you can head over to The Nose for even more of the good stuff in life.

THE NOSE WINE BAR

Cape Quarter, Dixon Street, De Waterkant
Mondays to Sundays, 11am till late (the kitchen closes at 10.30pm). Opening times on Sundays vary so call ahead
021 425-2200
www.thenose.co.za

tea at the nellie

AFTERNOON TEA AT THE MOUNT NELSON

The preferred haunt of the moneyed set (old money, not new), the Pink Nellie will always be the *grande dame* of Cape Town.

But, while not everyone can check in their Louis Vuitton for the night, it doesn't mean such style is beyond our grasp. Tea at the Nellie is an institution. Every afternoon, the overstuffed floral sofas are occupied by people listening to the piano player while genteelly sipping Lapsang Souchong and helping themselves to the sumptuous buffet – cucumber sandwiches, scones and jam, petits fours, steamed puddings and more. But it's the ambience that takes the proverbial cake.

**AFTERNOON TEA
AT THE MOUNT NELSON**
76 Orange Street, Gardens
Mondays to Sundays, 2.30pm till 5.30pm
021 483-1000

biltong and braaivleis

MORRIS'S

Droëwors, biltong and boerewors to quicken the pulse of the most avid carnivore can be found at Morris's. This butchery has been around for as long as anyone can remember, and Old Man Morris established a reputation that ensures that many Capetonians will buy their meat nowhere else, even if they do have to circle the block a few times before finding parking.

Morris's world-famous wors is the stuff of local legend, and, if meat's your thing, this green-and-white tiled establishment will have you salivating.

MORRIS'S
265 Long Street, CBD
Mondays to Fridays, 8.30am till 5.15pm,
Saturdays, 8.30am till 12pm
021 423-1766

the adams family

ONDERSTEUN HANDELAARS
AT SALT RIVER MARKET

No more pre-packaged, cellophane-wrapped veggies, no more queues at the checkout counters. If shopping at food and vegetable markets is good enough for the Naked Chef, then surely we should be looking out for our own markets? Fortunately, Ondersteun Handelaars at the Salt River Market has been around for years – four generations to be exact – and they'll still be around long after the latest food fad has come and gone.

Run by the Adams family, this fruit, vegetable and spice market is the real thing. Generations of customers have been served here and the Adams know each regular's family history – their favourite foods, what they prepare on special occasions and their culinary weaknesses.

Sisters Rumina and Zubaida and their father Yusuf preside over stacked boxes of brightly-coloured fruits and a wild assortment of vegetables. Here you will find celeriac, fennel, okra, sour figs (a Cape speciality), several types of mushrooms, chestnuts, Cape gooseberries, Kalahari truffles and all varieties of chilli. Ondersteun smells of freshly picked herbs, of ripe fruits, vanilla pods and oriental spices.

The Adams call this home; it's where they eat their breakfast and prepare their lunch, where they serve their regulars and help first-time visitors find the lemongrass, where they plan family feasts, where the spice rack hides the postcards from travelling customers and where their late mother's photo watches over them.

ONDERSTEUN HANDELAARS AT SALT RIVER MARKET
Salt River Market, off the circle at the start of Voortrekker Road
Mondays to Fridays, 8am till 6pm,
Saturdays, 7.30am till 4pm
021 448-1491

Body & Soul

SPIRIT · MIND · BELIEF

The mind is willing, but the flesh is weak. Can there be hope for the soul? Only in Cape Town, where holistic living is celebrated, meditation classes encouraged and contact details of spiritual advisors circulated. Perhaps it's the energy radiating from the mountain that causes this spiritual awareness, or maybe it's the strong pull of the ocean tides. Whatever it is, here, in the protective shadow of the mountain, your soul will find solace, your body will heal and your mind will find its inspiration.

being needled

DR LIN – ACUPUNCTURIST

M ost people don't like pain. And yet vast numbers regularly submit to needles. In an acupuncture sort of way. Why? Because apparently they didn't know how bad they felt until they started feeling better.

Acupuncture is the insertion of fine stainless steel needles into the body. This ancient Chinese techinique is said to unblock obstructions that hamper the natural circulation of energy through the body's meridians, stimulating and encouraging the body's healing abilities and promoting physical and emotional wellbeing.

Taiwanese-born Dr Feng-Chao Lin is pretty much a legend in this town. During visits to his practice you will hear remarkable stories of people overcoming ME, being relieved of backache for the first time in years or overcoming depression. Sinus sufferers and diabetics fill the waiting room, alongside those needing to stop smoking, lose weight or combat a drug habit. Doctors who practise conventional Western medicine refer patients to him; physiotherapists send him their no-hope patients. They are repeatedly astounded by what he achieves. His regulars whisper his name reverently and pass on his phone number to those in need.

Dr Lin is a highly skilled specialist who exudes a reassuring aura of confidence. He is an intuitive healer who is able to provide comfort and help where conventional Western medicine has often failed.

With his son Yukuan Lin, Dr Lin works from his home in Plumstead. You are expected to leave your shoes at the door. Chinese music plays in the background and you are quite likely to see Dr Lin practising Chinese characters on large, white sheets of paper. He is humble, pragmatic and firm, a man of few words. But those few words are measured: 'Suffering can transform itself into wisdom,' he says.

DR LIN — ACUPUNCTURIST
7 Pinehill Avenue, Plumstead
By appointment only
021 761-7742

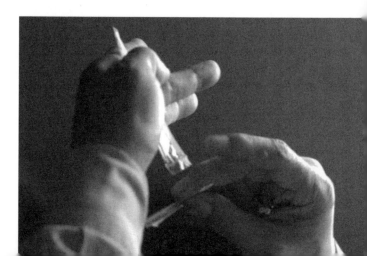

spiritual pursuits

CENTRE OF SPIRITUAL PHILOSOPHY

Every Thursday at 8pm an eclectic group of people gather to learn more about the spiritual realm. Sylvia Katz of the Centre of Spiritual Philosophy puts the programme together and every week people meet here to experience demonstrations of mediumship, or to discuss the Crop Circle phenomenon.

If this sort of thing isn't your usual buzz, but you are a little curious and would like to visit, you can rest assured that everyone there seems pretty normal. All you need is your R15 donation at the door and an open mind.

The Centre also offers half-hour meditation groups on Sundays (5pm), Tuesdays (2pm) and Wednesdays (6.15pm) and free spiritual healing on Mondays (6pm to 8.45pm).

CENTRE OF SPIRITUAL PHILOSOPHY
Ashby Manor, 242 High Level Road, Sea Point
021 439-6005 or 021 494-1879

stairway to heaven

ST GEORGE'S CATHEDRAL

S t George's Cathedral is a beautiful, imposing structure, but its reputation is that of a caring and involved parish. Archbishop Desmond Tutu wrote that '…as a site and focus of resistance against apartheid… St George's won the splendid accolade contained in the title "The People's Cathedral".'

It's a place not only to be visited on Sundays (although their 11am Masses on the last Sunday of the month are legendary), but also during the week.

The Cape Philharmonic Orchestra sometimes performs here and on Friday evenings you can listen to jazz performances in the Crypt.

ST GEORGE'S CATHEDRAL
Wale Street, CBD
021 424-7360
www.stgeorgescathedral.com

Crypt Restaurant
Mondays to Fridays, 8:30am till late,
Saturdays, 8:30am till 3pm

hey chi wow

HOLISTIC LIFESTYLE FAIR

This is not going to be everybody's cup of herbal tea: some Capetonians just don't believe in tarot, Reiki or aura-cleansing ceremonies. However a large portion of our community does embrace it all – and the monthly Holistic Lifestyle Fair at the Observatory Recreation Centre is where many practitioners and followers congregate.

The Fair is not only for adults; free-spirited kids can be found at the children's carnival and everyone is so easy-going that the odd one throwing a temper tantrum is really no cause for alarm. Here you can seek your soul's destiny... or find the perfect wheat-free muffin.

The more adventurous or spiritually inclined will head off to hear life readings. It may be the angel lady with butterflies in her hair who, with her pink, heart-shaped cards, holds the key to your future, or perhaps it is the sangoma who throws her bones and warns you of life's possible pitfalls. If these spiritual quests fall outside of your Calvinist framework, don't panic. In the therapy rooms you can experience aurasoma (colour healing), shiatsu or Indian head massage, aromatherapy and reflexology. They're done in communal rooms that are perhaps a little less private than one would wish, but the price is right and the clients appear not to care too much.

Should it be shopping you're after, you'll find yourself in a psychedelic heaven – hand-painted T-shirts, crystal balls, feng shui frogs, wind chimes, music for meditation, aromatherapy oils and an assortment of funky arts are all on sale. There's plenty of free patrolled parking and even something called an Orgasmatron. Now *there's* a very clever little invention!

HOLISTIC LIFESTYLE FAIR

Observatory Recreation Centre, off Lower Main and Station roads, Observatory
First Sunday of every month, 10am till 4pm
021 782-8882

turkish delight

LONG STREET POOL AND TURKISH BATHS

Margie Strydom presides over Cape Town's Turkish Baths on Ladies' Day. She's worked there for twenty-two years and takes no nonsense from anybody. She'll call you angel, reassure you that she's seen bodies of all shapes and sizes and suggest that you get on with it. So don't worry about not knowing the ropes – Margie will tell you exactly what and what not to do.

The first thing to do is to disrobe and wrap yourself in one of the purple City of Cape Town towels you will find in a small cubicle. This cubicle will be yours for the rest of your four-hour session. Next you're off to the hot room, where you can alternate between the even hotter sauna and the hotter-still steam room, where you can loofah and lather before hosing yourself down with icy water. Then you can plunge, naked as a jay bird, into a small freezing rectangular pool before returning to the hot room. Margie will call you when she feels you're ready for a massage, done on a marble slab with a wooden head-rest.

Think health here, not indulgence. The Turkish Bath is a cleansing process and not, as one would imagine, a wholly sensual indulgence – lack of privacy prohibits it, as does the slightly clinical atmosphere – but you do feel a sense of community with the women around you. And at R60 for the session you'll be hard-pressed to find a more afford-able way of experiencing something similar.

Men will have to do without the massage, but at R45 they shouldn't complain – the steam room beckons, the sauna's on and there's a wonderful swimming pool.

It's an old world institution with old world traditions but you'll leave feeling like a real Capetonian.

LONG STREET POOL
AND TURKISH BATHS
The mountain end of Long Street, CBD
Women: Mondays, Tuesdays, Thursdays and Saturdays
Men: Tuesdays, Wednesday, Fridays and Sundays
Open 7am to 7pm daily but it's best to call beforehand
021 400-3302

hair!

WIM COIFFEUR

In this small Sea Point salon, Wim van Zyl and the reformed street cat Coiffeur offer a haven to harassed clients and horrible hair. It's zen-like and stylishly simple, with none of the pretence of other salons.

Wim is a talented artist with an uncanny knowledge of what suits his clients; he is creative and practical and completely understands the relationships some have with their hair. But people go to Wim for more than just a hairstyle; here you're served fresh coffee and chocolate biscuits or sherry and Turkish Delight while waiting to be transformed. If you're looking for more than a haircut, this may be the place you've been searching for.

WIM COIFFEUR
Victoria Mansions, Shop 2, 119 Regent Road, Sea Point
Tuesdays to Saturdays but phone for an appointment
021 439-6131

107

under your skin

WILDFIRE — BODY ART

At either of Wildfire's two studios, you are as likely to wait in line next to a doctor wanting a nipple ring, a lawyer seeking scarification, an MP in search of something very private or a conservative-looking mom waiting to pay for her son's first tattoo.

Body art has come a long way since the days of crude anchors on ageing sailors. San designs, intricate Japanese symbols and the more popular brand names of modern day culture are admired, while glittering belly rings are the norm and hardly anyone worries about genital piercing. You can even, should you wish, have your tongue split. According to Jason at Wildfire, 'You have no idea what lurks beneath people's skin.'

And the health hazards? Minimal, if you're careful. Wildfire staff undergo rigorous training and sterilisation procedures are excellent. Don't go to some of the more dodgy outfits; hygiene and safety are not things you should be compromising on.

WILDFIRE — BODY ART
Body Piercing Clinic, Purple Turtle, 2nd level, corner of Long and Shortmarket streets, CBD
Tattoo Studio, 37 Burg Street, Greenmarket Square, CBD
021 422-0524

it's in the stars

VAL PAUL — SPIRITUAL COUNSELLOR

Val's melodious voice on the telephone will give you an inkling as to her gentle nature. She is a friend to her many clients; they guard her number jealously, giving it only to those they trust. We're breaking that unwritten code here because it may be that you were meant to see her. Do try, although you may have to wait a while as Val only occasionally takes on new clients.

Val is an astrologer with a strong psychic ability, and her intuition and guidance have helped many overcome difficult periods in their lives. If you are a horoscope-junkie, dashing from one clairvoyant to the next, then Val is not the woman for you. She is kind, yet firm, and her pragmatic approach and honesty will not appeal to those wanting crystals, incense and chanting. That's not her style.

To do a reading Val needs the date and preferably the time of your birth. Before the session, she will lay down a few ground rules: 'Don't expect everything just to "happen". While a lot will come about – I point out potential happenings – it is up to you to make the most of good opportunities and avoid the pitfalls.' She encourages you to use the information she gives you to make your life happier and more worthwhile, but Val is adamant that a reading is a only guide and that ultimately you shape your own destiny.

Val doesn't always tell you what you want to hear, although she does tell you as much as possible, with your best interests at heart. Her insights and intuition regarding emotional matters are astounding.

Some seek personal guidance, while other clients consult her on corporate matters; personnel, recruitment and business ventures. All in all, her clients are a varied bunch, but they have two things in common: they normally don't go in for this sort of things and they think of Val as a trusted friend.

VAL PAUL –
SPIRITUAL COUNSELLOR
Mouille Point
By appointment only
021 439-8255

calm

TIBETAN BUDDHIST MEDITATION CENTRE

The Tibetan Buddhist Meditation Centre's shrine room overlooks a tranquil suburban quad where sunbirds flit around and chimes tinkle in the breeze.

A wonderful friend told us about this centre. She has a calm and gentle aura and is a beautiful example of someone living well. This is where she hangs out.

Activities ranging from beginners' meditation courses to tantric compassion are on offer from Mondays to Fridays at 7pm, and retreats are held on Sundays, or for longer at out-of-town venues. Events on the Tibetan calendar are celebrated and Tibetan lamas and monks are sometimes guest teachers here. Cultural activities like thangka painting (intricate paintings on silk) are offered and the centre's shop is well stocked with books and devotional items. The Centre also arranges pilgrimages to India, Tibet and Nepal every two years.

TIBETAN BUDDHIST MEDITATION CENTRE
6 Morgenrood Road, Kenilworth
021 761-2978

aloha

LOUISE KLEU – KA HUNA
MASSAGE PRACTITIONER

A massage is always good; it relaxes you, it feels great and you can justify the expense and time by thinking of its potential health benefits. But don't go mistaking one massage for another. There's a world of difference and Ka huna massage may well be the ultimate – think blissful island luxury indulgence as opposed to a package holiday.

Louise Kleu is a Ka huna Bodywork Therapist and specialises in what she calls Transformational Massage. Originating in Polynesia, Ka huna is a complete healing system aimed at restoring balance and harmony to body, mind and spirit. A Ka huna treatment overwhelms the mind with sensation as the practitioner uses intuitive movements, loud breathing and rhythm. With the use of hands and arms in dance-like movements that mirror the ebb and flow of the ocean, it can, at times, almost be described as an energetic massage. But this does not fully convey the entire experience.

To Louise, music is an integral part of the treatment but, if you're thinking whale music and baroque, you're way off track. For an hour and a half, Louise focuses all her energy on her client; it is an intensely emotional experience that involves a certain degree of trust between practitioner and client. It is here that Louise's gentleness and honesty come to the fore, putting you completely at ease. In a warm, candle-lit healing room surrounded by music, she approaches her work with an open heart and believes 'in the individual's potential to transform and create the life they want and to make a positive difference in the world.'

LOUISE KLEU – KA HUNA MASSAGE PRACTITIONER
Hout Bay
By appointment only
084 318-2631

feel free to float

VANILLA FLOAT — FLOTATION THERAPY

This slightly surreal therapy is somewhat strange… and incredibly relaxing. It works like this: for sixty minutes you float in a light- and soundproof tank. The water is heated to body temperature and huge quantities of salt ensure that you are able to float. Lying in this capsule, deprived of two of your senses, you can either reach an altered state of consciousness or, like ourselves, fall into a deep sleep (which is also good).

Vanilla Float is a wonderful urban oasis. There are massages and beauty treatments to be had at Vanilla Essence and if, after floating, caffeine calls, you can stop off for a seriously good cappuccino at the Vanilla Café.

VANILLA FLOAT — FLOTATION THERAPY
The Coach House, 117 Hatfield Street, Gardens
Mondays to Fridays, 8.30am till 5pm but make an appointment
021 461-6982

powerful praise

UZUKO LENKONZO YAMANYANGE CHURCH

A lone voice broke the silence and then the voices of women rose up in praise. In a small shack church in Philippi, one cold and wet Sunday morning, the Lord witnessed his people glorifying His name. The power of worship in a place where they, who have so little, praise Him for so much, is palpable and a visit to Uzuko Lenkonzo Yamanyange Church is a humbling, deeply spiritual experience.

Here, a mere twenty-minute drive from some of the more forbidding churches of wealthier parishes in neighbouring suburbs, you can worship with the people of Philippi. The community built the Home of Our Lord, and they offered all that they could. Wind-torn flags and murals of the Madonna front the church, while the inside is a celebration of colour as fabrics in hues of magenta, royal blues, reds, greens and shiny white cover the corrugated walls. The lushness of ornamentation and colour is at odds with the austerity of a church where women cover their heads and young virgins wear white veils. In other churches the colourful altar and oddly matched religious relics would look out of place, but here the large neon cross, plastic flowers, cut-out images of Christ and mismatched light-fittings mirror the joyous generosity of the worshippers.

Before the service, taped classical music is played, creating an air of sombre formality broken only by someone ringing a bell through the streets, calling people to worship. The classical sounds are in sharp contrast to the powerful Xhosa hymns sung during the service. Then, hands are clapped, mothers move with their babies tied to their backs, male voices are lowered in prayer, and joyful harmonies drown out the sounds of a mournful wind.

Jan Jasone, our guide, was one of the church's founding members and he translates for his visitors, giving insights into this remarkable place. Visiting with him as your guide does not feel intrusive or voyeuristic. We left with the sound of voices raised in harmonious praise. The sincerity and spiritual strength of these worshippers touched something deep within each of us.

UZUKO LENKONZO YAMANYANGE CHURCH
Philippi, but book to go with Jan Jasone or Debbie Bird
of New World Inc
Sunday mornings
021 790-8825

back off

DR NICOLE DESCOINS – CHIROPRACTOR

Sometimes referred to as the 'pain and strain doctors', chiropractors – who iron out kinks in backs and necks – are often regarded as a last resort. Along comes the petite Dr Nicole Descoins, saviour to sufferers.

She is dedicated, careful and hugely successful. Her business card is passed around in offices and her telephone number is whispered among desperate mums with colicky, fretful babies. She sorts out back and neck problems and has a remarkable reputation for treating newborns. Sceptical paediatricians and concerned parents have been amazed at the results she gets. Not only do the babies Nicole treats stop crying, but they love the gentle way she handles their tiny bodies.

Screaming baby, painful shoulder, aching neck? You really don't need to suffer.

DR NICOLE DESCOINS – CHIROPRACTOR
28 Deer Park Drive, Highlands Estate, Vredehoek
By appointment only
021 462-7707

BRUCE TAIT PG 132

Collectibles

RETRO · BOOKS · ARTIFACTS

The things we value and collect tell much of who we are. Some treasures have a monetary worth; others are simply valued for sentimental reasons. And who is to judge or put a price on that which we love? But it's the search for a specific object that will bring you almost as much pleasure as the actual discovery – you will meet people passionate about the past, and discover treasure troves more tempting than any modern emporium.

time stands still

BEINKINSTADT

In 1903, in an area that was once the heart of Cape Town's Jewish community, Moses Beinkinstadt opened a shop specialising in Judaica. One hundred years and three generations later, Beinkinstadt is run by Moses's grandson, Michael Padowich, and his wife Fay. They sell everything from yarmulkes, prayer shawls, candlesticks, wine goblets, challah covers and mezuzoth to books, some of which are still the same stock that Moses Beinkinstadt once ordered.

The shop does not appear to have changed much since its inception. It still boasts the original shop-fittings, the same desk that Michael's father and grandfather used, and the cash register is the same one that rang up the purchases of seventy years ago. The wooden floors creak, and the opening of a drawer may cause a soft puff of dust to catch the light before settling on the old wooden counter.

125

A visit to Beinkinstadt is a rite of passage, and many an urban sophisticate fondly recalls making his Barmitzvah purchases from here. Beinkinstadt has served generations of the city's Jewish community and its owners know the history of the many Lithuanian Jewish families who first settled in the area. Here, there is a sense of permanence in a fast-paced world. While you may want to rush in and buy what you need, you will find yourself overcome by nostalgia and wanting to chat to the Padowiches about almost-forgotten people and places.

BEINKINSTADT
38 Canterbury Street, CBD
Mondays to Fridays, 9am till 5pm
021 461-2431

treasure hunt

MILNERTON FLEAMARKET

Bordering the railway line and the industrial area in a notoriously windy area, the Milnerton Fleamarket is hardly one of the Peninsula's more picturesque markets. But it is, according to those in the know, one of the best.

In between the biltong stands and cut-price vitamin stalls, amid the old car parts and broken light fittings, there hides treasure. Some dealers claim they've discovered original Clarice Cliff here, while another swears on his mother's life that he bought a piece of Lalique for R15!

Go in seach of treasure early in the morning. That's when Marcus Brewster goes...

MILNERTON FLEAMARKET
Paarden Eiland, Milnerton
Saturdays and Sundays, 7am till 3pm

crystal etc

DELOS

In a Moroccan-blue building on the edge of Bo-Kaap stands Delos. The name was not business partners' Jerome and Jason's first choice, but, when they opened eight years ago, the Council refused to allow them to call their shop Jack & Jesus.

Jerome and Jason have excellent taste, which is reflected in the eclectic collection of treasures that they stock. They have the largest selection of crystal chandeliers anywhere in South Africa; Venetian mirrors reflect hunting trophies; African animal horns and select pieces of antique furniture are on display – all beautiful and waiting to be purchased by someone who appreciates their charm. Here at Delos, antiques are not the sole property of dusty, draughty old manor houses; they are objects with a memory of times past, but as suited to the present day and modern designer homes as they ever were in their previous lives.

129

You will find Delos is neither pretentious nor stuffy, and that the rather gorgeous men who own it evidently love what they do; chandeliers are repaired, advice is given and there is a general sense of creative and stylish mayhem.

DELOS
140 Buitengracht Street, Bo-Kaap
Mondays to Fridays,
9am till 5pm,
Saturdays, 9am till 1pm
021 424-7573 or
021 422-0334

treasures & tat

THE LONG STREET ANTIQUE ARCADE

If you're not of the less-is-more school, you'll love this arcade of twelve antique shops and one very good café. Each shop has its own speciality, be it glassware, jewellery, military memorabilia, or vintage clothes.

It's easy to get stuck in Shop 5, where Bob Hayward has his collection of medical, scientific and engineering tools. He also has – and, damn it, we should really keep this secret – a selection of old South African signs and advertising boards. We couldn't resist the silver foil Voortrekker Monument, but others will be captivated by the more sane objects in his collection.

THE LONG STREET ANTIQUE ARCADE
127 Long Street, CBD
Mondays to Fridays, 9am till 5pm,
Saturdays, 9am till 2pm
072 213-4807

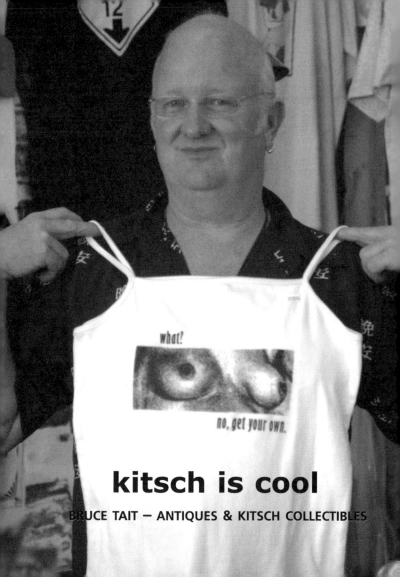

kitsch is cool

BRUCE TAIT — ANTIQUES & KITSCH COLLECTIBLES

We're not so sure about the presence of antiques in this over-the-top shop, but that it is an altar to high kitsch is certain. Bruce Tait has a loyal following: Capetonians regularly wander in to see what's new. They buy Brett Murray's desirably fabulous boogie lights, Elvis profiles, red-hot chillis, flying saucers or even a Sacred Heart.

This is where you are most likely to find a Tretchi print, a faded old South African flag, banana-shaped string lights, Afrikaans condoms – *Vir Die Groot Meneer* – snow-domes, religious icons to appeal to the most devout collector of kitsch and pre-1994 South African memorabilia. Bruce Tait also stocks an array of T-shirts with subversive slogans that will have you standing out in the crowd.

Bring along your sense of humour, as well as your wallet; you will be tempted by a wide assortment of stuff that you once mocked and now cannot live without.

BRUCE TAIT – ANTIQUES & KITSCH COLLECTIBLES
Buitenkloof Centre, 8 Kloof Street, Gardens
Mondays to Fridays, 10am till 6pm,
Saturdays and Sundays, 9.30am till 2pm
021 422-1567

the antique road show

KALK BAY ANTIQUE STRIP

On weekends city-slickers flock to Kalk Bay to experience the bohemian atmosphere of this seaside village and to snoop around the boutiques and antiques shops that line Main Road.

The joy is in the treasure hunt atmosphere of it all. Looking for vintage railway tea sets? You'll find them here, along with complete sets of crockery, from Royal Albert to pieces from the 1950s. Wood-panelled shops sell antique books, others specialise in nautical goods and a little kitchen shop, tucked away in an alley, displays old cake tins and other nostalgic kitchenware to quicken the heart of chefs and sentimental folk alike.

In between shops, you can rest in cafés and restaurants. Look out for the pancake place, the by-now-famous bakery, and that little shop that sells everything from African artifacts to bright pink, feathered lampshades.

KALK BAY ANTIQUE STRIP
A few of the shops you'll find on, or just off,
Main Road, Kalk Bay are:
Cape to Cairo, 021 788-6348
Quagga Art & Books, 021 788-2752
The Cook's Room, 021 788-6348
The Whatnot & China Town, 021 788-1823
Opening times are usually Mondays to Saturdays,
9.30am till 5pm

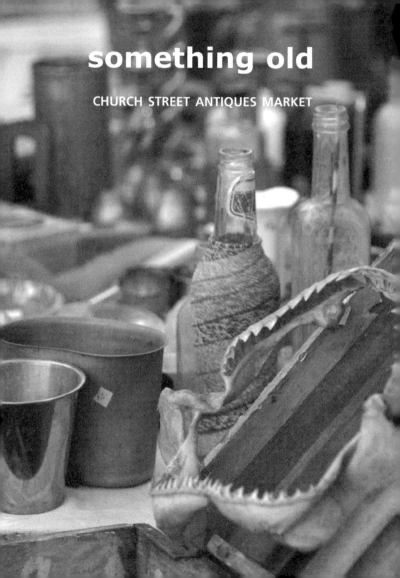

something old

CHURCH STREET ANTIQUES MARKET

In beautiful tree-lined Church Street, you will find shiny bits of crystal, old Kewpie dolls, 1950s glass ashtrays, railway coffeepots, stamps, black and white 1930s erotic prints, some nonsense and a whole lot of treasure.

The traders here are an interesting lot who are keen to help; even if you're not a serious buyer, they'll still chat and impart their knowledge.

There are antique shops and art galleries (the AVA is here) on either side of the cobbled road, as well as the legendary Café Mozart, where you can get really good coffee and great food. You're likely to find yourself spending more time here than you thought you would.

CHURCH STREET ANTIQUES MARKET
Church Street, CBD
Mondays to Saturdays, 9am till 2pm

a blast from
the past

KARIZMA

There is a rage for 50s and 60s furniture and Karizma is where you'll find almost anything that your retro little heart desires.

There are few places that stock a more comprehensive array of furniture and accessories. They have an impressive and valuable selection of original furniture, with a strong leaning towards art deco. For some, the 1950s kitchen cabinets will tug at the heartstrings; for others of the pro-smoking ilk what better than a heavy, ornate glass ashtray?

According to the charming Ronnie Fellows who runs the shop, 'Style is a language of many dialects.' This is as good a place as any to brush up on your pronunciation.

KARIZMA
44 Chiappini Street, De Waterkant
Mondays to Fridays, 9am till 5pm,
Saturdays, 9am till 1pm
021 421-7070

139

things of yesteryear

yesteryear

HOTCHI-WITCHI

The strange-sounding name will lure you into Hotchi-Witchi, a Victorian home on Kloof Street. The impressive selection of stuff from yesteryear will keep you there.

Toy trains, model car collections, old-fashioned transistor radios and an outstanding collection of old cameras – most of them are of the 1950s variety, but some go back a hundred years. Every room in the house is filled to capacity; one is full of old kitchen-ware, and another is stuffed full of fragile crockery and glassware. In the passage you'll find a collection of old children's books that will bring back a flood of memories.

Take your grandmother, or go alone and honour her memory.

HOTCHI-WITCHI
90 Kloof Street, Gardens
Mondays to Fridays, 9am till 5pm,
Saturdays, 9am till 1pm
021 422-3811

paper chase

CLARKE'S BOOKS

There are people in this world who fold pages in a book to mark the page they last read. They are probably the same sort of people who will ask to borrow a much-loved book of yours and then never return it. These are not the sort of people who will shop at Clarke's Books.

This literary wonderland in Long Street is reserved for true book-lovers. The shelves are laden, the wooden floors creak and there are deco chairs for you to curl up in while you page through your finds. No sparkly, commercial bookshop this – Clarke's is how bookshops were always meant to be.

Henrietta Dax presides over this legendary establishment and, when she is not travelling through southern Africa looking for rare books, she can be found among her beloved tomes, giving invaluable advice to earnest literary types from all over the world.

CLARKE'S BOOKS
211 Long Street, CBD
Mondays to Fridays, 9am till 5pm,
Saturdays, 9am till 1pm
021 423-5739
www.clarkesbooks.co.za

MINCE PG 160

Show Time

CHARACTER · FETISH · FUN

Cape Town is a little off-beat. It's kinder to say quirky, rather than odd, and we really would prefer being called interesting. This end of Africa is a melting pot of cultures and somehow all tastes are catered for. So, if you're looking for culture, you'll find concert recitals in cathedrals. Something edgy? Try being suspended from hooks in a crowded nightclub wearing only a small leather two-piece. Rhythm divine? Grab a djembe and drum into the early hours of the morning. As a wise old someone must have said, 'Your only limitation is your imagination.'

ag, darling!

EVITA SE PERRON

She is a national treasure, the most famous white woman in Africa. With her floral dresses, political ambitions and powerful friends, Evita Bezuidenhout is the nation's darling.

Her alter ego, Pieter-Dirk Uys, is perhaps less popular in certain political circles; he is the man who campaigned to have President Thabo Mbeki and Minister Manto Tshabalala-Msimang appear before the International Court of Justice on counts of genocide because of their stance on HIV/Aids. He has always been, and will remain, a fearless champion of the oppressed.

When Cape Town boy Pieter-Dirk left the city and made the small town of Darling home, Tannie Evita set up camp at the Perron. Now the old train station is a Temple of High Kitsch, filled with doilies, Verwoerd *staan-lampies*, old parliamentary portraits, flags and Whites Only signs.

147

Darling is only a short drive from Cape Town and well worth the trip. You can enjoy traditional bobotie, melktert and koeksisters in Tannie Evita's Pantry, buy arts and crafts shop at Evita's A en C and watch a South African icon at work. Pieter-Dirk's acclaimed shows run regularly and change frequently (so it's best to view the website for the latest information). They vary from *Dekaffirnated* to *Tannie Evita Praat Kaktus* – Evita Bezuidenhout's legendary state-of-the-nation address.

Pieter-Dirk Uys once described himself as a 'middle-aged, gay, Afrikaans, Jewish, *vetgat, kaalkop, katmal* stage manager, who wears dresses and acts'. He's so more than that. He is our conscience and our sanity.

EVITA SE PERRON
Darling Station, Darling
Tuesdays to Sundays
022 492-2831 or 022 492-2851
www.evita.co.za

ELECTIONS & ERECTIONS
Read Pieter-Dirk Uys's 'memoir of fear and fun'
Published by Zebra Press
R139.95

laugh!

CAPE COMEDY COLLECTIVE

The CCC taught the Mother City to laugh at itself. The Cape Comedy Collective falls under the banner of South African Monster Productions (SAMP), headed up by the indomitable Sam Pearce and her very funny man Mark Sampson. Together, this loosely-banded group of comedians shed some light on our many idiosyncracies: why 'now' means 'later', the complexities of specific hair textures and the unspoken township code, to name a few.

SAMP comedians perform at venues around town and their material is always topical and edgy. The comedy scene is an evolving animal, so it's best to go onto their website and see what they're up to. If they're not selling SA to the Brits, or being mentioned in the *New York Times*, they're probably taking the piss at a venue near you.

CAPE COMEDY COLLECTIVE
021 789-1665
www.samp.co.za

calling elvis

ERNEST MACDONALD – ELVIS IMPERSONATOR

Elvis is alive and well and living in Sea Point. He's also running a very successful fleet of taxis and owns a couple of helicopters.

Ernest MacDonald is an Elvis impersonator – one of the best kind. No tired, sweat-soiled polyester costumes for this man. Like the King himself, Mr Mac enjoys the finer things in life. His pink Cadillac with Elvis plates, flashy outfits, and sparkling white boots tell of a man who pays tribute to a legend with the utmost respect. His performances are worthy of one of the greatest rock icons of our time and those who have seen him on stage use words like electrifying.

Ernest MacDonald is something of an enigma, a hard-line businessman, an animal rights activist and Elvis impersonator. He will perform at weddings, birthdays and fundraising events and, while he doesn't charge for his performance, he does expect you to donate something to animal welfare organisations. And don't go skimping on that donation: Ernest is no cheap Elvis entertainer and pays a worthy tribute to the King of Excess.

ERNEST MACDONALD – ELVIS IMPERSONATOR
021 462-3723
Catch Ernest in action at his day job, at the The Graceland Workshop panel beaters, 62 Newmarket Street, CBD

in suspense

JASON MACDONALD – SUSPENSION

Imagine a club in Observatory where a woman has hooks inserted in her body, is hoisted up by her flesh and is left hanging there for thirty minutes. She does this because she wants to.

Suspension, as this ritual is known, is body piercing taken to the extreme, and Jason MacDonald is the man who facilitates it. Quietly well-spoken and very knowledgeable about the art he practises, Jason is laid-back, yet in control. He inspires confidence – he would have to, considering what people ask him to do to them.

Suspension takes about an hour to set up. It is a clinical procedure: Jason works out the distribution of weight and hooks, the skin is cleaned and the position of the hooks is marked on your flesh. The hooks are inserted with surgical precision, but, strangely, there is no blood (this has something to do with the pressure on the flesh).

153

Then you are hoisted up and suspended above the crowd. The system is interconnected; if one hook fails, the suspension system will pull the hooks in different directions. Causing damage, obviously.

Why would anyone do this? According to Jason, some see it as a rite of passage. Others do it to conquer their fears. 'It's pretty hard-core; being lifted by your flesh is terrifying, and it does hurt.' Jason also believes that doing it in front of people is a quest for validation.

And for the onlooker? 'It's a bit like horror movies; people are curious, they like to be shocked, they want to see how it's done, like to see how someone goes through a process which is in fact life-changing.'

Suspensions can be arranged for events from rock concerts to private functions. If you're up for it, that is.

JASON MACDONALD – SUSPENSION
Wherever you like
Call Wildfire and they'll put you in contact with Jason
021 422-0524

dancing on the table

THROW A PARTY ON TOP OF TABLE MOUNTAIN

How about it? No queues at the cable car for you or your friends, and the world – or at least Cape Town – at your feet for the night. So it may cost you, but you're worth it, aren't you?

The very nice folks at Table Mountain Aerial Cableway Company have it all worked out and will happily arrange everything you need in order to hold your own party on the mother of all mountains.

The view from the top is superb, you'll have millions of lights below and the stars almost within touching distance. It's really so much nicer than the local town hall…

THROW A PARTY ON TOP OF TABLE MOUNTAIN
On top of Table Mountain, of course
Speak to the Functions Co-ordinator
021 424-0015
www.tablemountain.net

the real
movie magic

THE LABIA CINEMA

A true Cape Town institution, the Labia is the oldest independent art-repertory cinema in the country. And, while the seats in some of the theatres may not be the most comfortable in town, the film selection is always excellent.

The Labia is the usual venue for the more intellectual movies on circuit and occasional film festivals. Sometimes you see them advertised, but mostly it's by word of mouth or the A4 sheets you'll find at surrounding shops and cafés that you'll find out what's on show.

Originally the Italian Embassy's ballroom, the building was inaugurated as a theatre by Princess Labia in 1949. The name still causes smirks among those not in the know and the rest of us all have a Labia story to tell. One highly-regarded journalist would like her ashes scattered in Screen 1. A well-known comedian, overcome by a case of the late night munchies, once took the Labia staff Tip Tin, along with his armful of chocolates, cooldrink and chips, into the theatre by mistake. And then there's the legend of another journalist, the Loud Popcorn Eater and the can of pepper spray...

While you are waiting for your movie to start, you can people-watch on the terrace outside below the neon sign, proudly proclaiming the theatre's name. There's also always plenty of film-buff conversation as well as some straight talk about the screenings.

The wooden refreshment counter is better than that at any commercial cinema, and the popcorn is served in brown paper bags. The Labia even has a liquor license, so on weekends, when it's crowded and the fashionable set queue alongside arty intellectuals, you can take your whisky into the theatre. On weekday mornings you may have the luxury of having a screening room to yourself, where you can drink hot coffee and eat warm sweet pastries from the cinema café.

THE LABIA CINEMA

68 Orange Street and Kloof Street, Gardens
Mondays to Sundays
021 424-5927
www.labia.co.za

classic cape town

CAPE PHILHARMONIC ORCHESTRA
AND CAPE TOWN CONCERT SERIES

It's not all beach and brawn at the southern end of Africa. When the concerts season starts, Capetonians flock together in anticipation of some serious music in exciting venues.

The Cape Philharmonic Orchestra holds regular concerts with acclaimed national and international artists at various venues, from the Artscape Theatre Centre to City Hall or St George's Cathedral. The Concert Series consists of monthly events at the Baxter in Rosebank.

It's well worth attending; not only are the musicians world-class, but it's no use screaming about lack of arts funding if you don't put your money where your mouth is.

CAPE PHILHARMONIC ORCHESTRA
AND CAPE TOWN CONCERT SERIES
021 410-9809 for the Cape Philharmonic Orchestra
021 439-7663 for the Cape Town Concert Series
www.ctconcerts.co.za

what a drag

MINCE

The divine Lili Slaptsilli (aka Clive Allardyce) and Kieron Legacy (aka Martin van Staden) have brought lashings of glamour to Main Road, Green Point, for the past eight years.

Mince is the ultimate in drag acts – slick, sexy and wickedly witty. With legs and couture to die for, these cocks in frocks strut their stuff to an appreciative audience. Here, you'll see the city at its unprejudiced best – lipstick lesbians, sturdy boerseuns, Cape Town kugels, moffies and straights, all having one hell of a time.

Their material evolves with every performance and no two shows are alike. The designer duo perform classic caberet interspersed with self-deprecating one-liners and some seriously funny asides. God help you should you be wearing Birkenstocks – the girls will rip you to pieces!

On Broadway is a fabulous venue, where you can enjoy dinner and a show and stay for drinks long after Lili and Kieron have taken off their make-up and wigs and put on their Levi's.

MINCE
On Broadway, 21 Somerset Road, De Waterkant Village
021 418-8338
www.onbroadway.co.za

a night on the town

TOWNSHIP MUSIC TOUR

The word 'shebeen' is derived from an eighteenth century Anglo-Irish word meaning 'mugful'. Shebeens are found in Ireland, Scotland and the townships of southern Africa. Originally unlicensed establishments selling illicit home-brewed liquor, today they are places where communities gather, parties are held and where the drink is generally cheaper than anywhere else. They are also where those who haven't made adequate provision for a late night party can buy alcohol long after other bottle stores have closed.

Non-township dwellers might at first be wary of visiting a shebeen, but, as with any other establishment, you go where you feel welcome, either with friends who are regulars or with people who know the area well. Debbie Bird and Jan Jasone from New World Inc are just such people. They specialise in township music tours and with them you will experience a whole new exciting culture. A typical tour might include a workshop on the instruments of southern Africa, traditional dancing, African story telling, a traditional African meal and a visit to a local shebeen for a drum circle and great township jazz, marimba or kwela. You might even be lucky enough to meet Dizu Plaatjies, founder of Amampondo marimba band, who lectures indigenous music at the University of Cape Town's Department of Ethnomusicology. Dizu is a wealth of information regarding traditional ways. His Aunt Madocini is a national treasure – one of a handful of people who can sing in split tones.

If you're hesitant about a tour, fearing that it's voyeuristic or exploitative, don't be. These tours show the fun, positive side of township tourism. You will experience the wealth of a unique cultural heritage, discover talented musicians and artists and emerge with a strong sense of the spirit of entrepreneurship.

TOWNSHIP MUSIC TOUR
Call Jan Jasone or Debbie Bird at New World Inc for
a tailormade tour
021 790-8825

partying with predators

PARTY AT THE TWO OCEANS AQUARIUM

It could be a scene straight out of a James Bond movie: tuxedos and evening gowns, a great jazz band, couples dancing beneath the watchful eyes of ragged tooth sharks.

In the movie, of course, there would be the dramatic scene where the glass walls of the predator tank crack. But happily, in the real world, that's not going to happen. Here the magic of the setting and the wow factor are within your reach. The Two Oceans Aquarium is a wonderful venue for the most amazing parties, whether you choose to party with predators, or keep company with friendlier forms of marine life, the choice is yours.

PARTY AT THE TWO OCEANS AQUARIUM
Dock Road, V&A Waterfront
Speak to the Functions Co-ordinator on 021 418-3823
www.aquarium.co.za

flavours flour & fun

LIVE AT THE OLYMPIA BAKERY

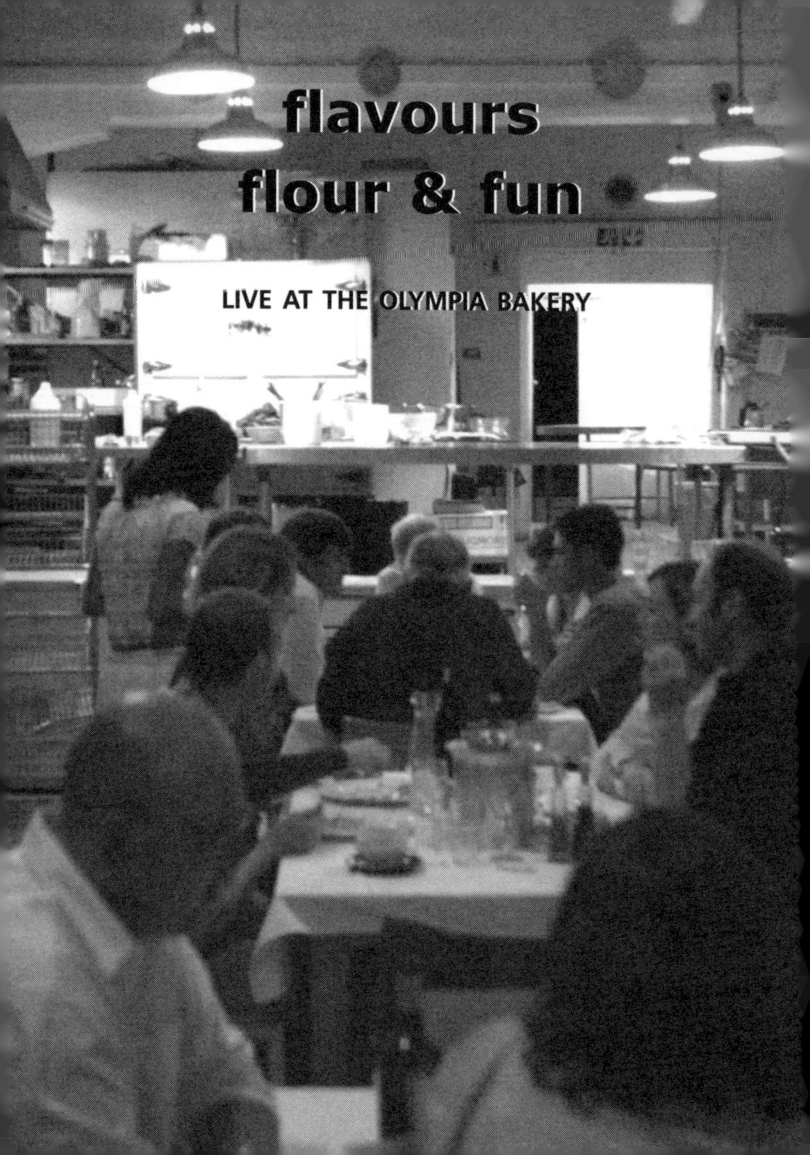

The Olympia Café & Deli is everybody's favourite funky hangout and they're prepared to queue for it. The food is excellent – think fresh fish, mussels with garlic cream sauce, chicken with cashew nuts and decadent desserts – and the ambience is laid-back and stylishly bohemian. But the main attraction is the bread. Oh heavens, the bread is pure manna!

So it is only right that the bakery where that bread is made is celebrated. Which is where Live at The Olympia Bakery comes in. At night, the cavernous bakery behind the café is transformed into a large diningroom; the industrial lights are dimmed slightly and the flour is hurriedly wiped up, but the ovens and large stainless steel preparation tables remain. A gorgeous dinner, with an impressive wine list, is served before diners move on to the tiny theatre at the back. Here, in a small space with surprisingly comfortable red chairs, reviews, intimate concerts and plays are performed by the talented likes of Nicholas Ellenbogen, Liz Szymczak, Jeroen Kranenburg and Godfrey Johnson. After the performance, guests wander back to their tables to enjoy their dessert, while the bakers fire up their ovens, roll out the dough and semi-patiently wait for you to finish so that they can get on with the business of baking for the next morning.

But, theatre types and gourmands being what they are, the lingering and chatting and drinking lasts longer than you might expect, mostly because you won't want the magic to end.

LIVE AT THE OLYMPIA BAKERY
Olympia Bakery Theatre
Corner of Boyes Drive and Main Road, Kalk Bay
073 220-5430

Olympia Café and Deli
Corner of Boyes Drive and Main Road, Kalk Bay
021 788-6396

playtime

SHAKESPEARE IN THE PARK

Pack the picnic basket and chilled bubbly and head for
Maynardville Park to learn the difference between
your wherefores and where art thous.

Every summer Artscape and the Maynardville
Theatre Trust present a production of one of William
Shakespeare's works. The shows are lavish and fun, and
Capetonians flock to get tickets. The grounds fill with
groups of people drinking wine and feasting on
pre-performance picnics as the sun sets on the park.

Then they take their seats in the open-air theatre
where, wrapped in blankets, they watch traditional plays
unfold in new and exciting ways. With the stars twinkling
above and under the watchful eye of the Bard himself's
statue, the city's theatre luvvies strut their stuff, keeping
an always-appreciative audience enthralled.

SHAKESPEARE IN THE PARK
Maynardville Open-Air Theatre, Main Road, Wynberg
Performances run from mid-January to end February
Artscape-Dial-A-Seat on 021 421-7695

beating the blues

THE DRUM CAFÉ

The Drum Café is not where you go for a quiet night out. Rather it's the sort of place where you're expected to go wild – the primeval instincts kick in once you get your hands on the djembe drum.

Drumming at the Drum Café is both a musical event and a bonding session. On Monday, Wednesday and Friday nights they offer classes ranging from beginners' lessons to advanced classes in the intricate traditional rhythms of South, Central and West Africa. You could find yourself drumming with over two hundred people.

If you prefer something more intimate, Catherine Welsh facilitates drumming circles. She believes drumming induces an alpha brainwave state associated with stress release, mental clarity and enhanced creativity. If you're nervous about it being a whole lot of bohemian types and hippies, relax – perfectly nice lawyers, accountants and commodity traders are into this sort of thing too.

THE DRUM CAFÉ
32 Glynn Street, Gardens
021 461-1305
www.drumcafe.co.za

Catherine Welsh on 021 686-3872
www.drummingsa.co.za

private pleasures

CINE 12

If you've ever wanted your own private screening room where you and the rest of your brat pack can hang out and watch movies, your prayers have been answered.

The lavish Twelve Apostles Hotel (spectacular seaviews, over-the-top suites, pet-friendly accommodation policy) has a fabulous alternative to the usual mass cinema experience. Cine 12 Dinner Evenings consist of a special three-course dinner, followed by a film of your choice in a super-luxurious sixteen-seat private screening room. To ensure an evening that's all yours, get six friends together, choose your flick from the hotel's library of two hundred and fifty-plus DVDs and settle into the plush red leather seats to enjoy superb Dolby surround sound and a state-of-the-art flat screen.

Naturally, there's a popcorn and sweets station and during interval hot chocolate, thick milkshakes and Magnum icecreams are served. This is the way you were always meant to watch *Casablanca*.

CINE 12 DINNER EVENINGS
The Twelve Apostles Hotel, Victoria Road, Camps Bay
021 437-9000
www.12apostleshotel.com

is becoming a...

Children under 12 and Natives.

...gular African patrons have deeply resented...

unceremoniously turned out of the theatre by the attendant...

We know that it is a governmental policy to sow dis...

and race-hatred amongst the different sections of the Non-

but we did not expect to see such a policy reflected eve...

picture houses. Of course we are aware that the usual

and that the Management therefore cannot help itself

excuse does not hold wat... for the Board of Censors

force any company to ... or hire ...ch films as are

Heritage

HISTORY · CULTURE · IDENTITY

History books will tell you about our city's past, but it is its people who will enrich your life with the telling of their stories. The wealth of our heritage lies within the hearts of the people of Cape Town. In the District Six Museum lies our shame and sadness, on Robben Island we find the spirit of forgiveness and, in the optimism of the flower sellers and the street wisdom of the bergies, we find the true picture of what it means to be from these parts.

the big bang

THE NOON GUN

Zapiro, South Africa's foremost cartoonist, immortalised both the laid-back attitude of Capetonians as well as the importance that the Noon Gun plays in our daily lives in a cartoon entitled *Life in Cape Town*. A woman exclaims: 'The Noon Gun! I'm late for my appointment!', to which her friend replies: 'Relax it's only 11.30... probably just a bomb.' That was in August 2000 and political times have changed, but the role the Noon Gun plays has not.

When the cannon is fired at exactly midday every afternoon (bar one) of the week, Capetonians automatically check their watches. We're hardly aware that we do it but it's a quirky collective habit that's been going for over a hundred years.

It's well worth going to the source of the noise. There are two guns up on the hill (one is a spare in case the other does not fire) and one and a half kilos of gunpowder is used each day. On some days you can see the smoke from the cannon in the city below and the noise is always deafening.

Originally fired to provide passing ships (and residents) with the correct time, the Noon Gun is operated by the South African Navy. Get there by 11.30am in order to meet Chief Petty Officer Dudley Malgas who has fired the gun every day, except for Sundays and public holidays, for the past eight years. He has a wealth of information and is keen to share his knowledge with those interested enough to be there on time.

There are two routes to the Noon Gun: one takes you past the clearly-marked Noon Gun Tea Room and Restaurant, but from here you have to climb a rather steep hill – it's about a ten-minute walk. Should you be a little lazy, or more cautious, use the route described below, where there's plenty of parking near the site.

THE NOON GUN

Military Road, Signal Hill (follow the signs from corner of Bloem & Buitengracht streets)
Mondays to Saturdays, 11.30am
021 787-1257

the iconic island

ROBBEN ISLAND

LIFE BUOYS

Robben Island is hardly a secret, but we simply had to include it. If you haven't been, do go, and, if you have, take someone who hasn't.

Here, we had the privilege of meeting Eddie Daniels (prisoner number 804/64) who served his fifteen-year sentence on the island in the company of Nelson Mandela, Walter Sisulu, Ahmed Kathrada and others. He's an inspiring man, kind and wise, and he gave us a frank and moving account of the years he spent here. When asked how he could bear coming back to the island he answers that it's 'because we won the war; our morals and values triumphed'.

Facing the lime quarry, with the sun's sharp reflection in his eyes, he pays tribute to his fellow prisoners who helped him achieve his matriculation certificate and two degrees.

Daniels also speaks of the moments of joy amid the suffering. Standing in the old Punishment Block listening to him speak, it is hard to comprehend the resilience of the human spirit. It is even harder to comprehend the enormity of forgiveness.

Should you want to read Eddie Daniels's book, *There & Back – Robben Island 1964–1979*, Mr Brandt, a former prison warden, will help you find it at the small bookshop at the Nelson Mandela Gateway.

Another former prisoner who has written an account of his ten years on Robben Island and who is available for tours is Indres Naidoo. His book, *Island in Chains*, can also be found at the bookshop. This is not to say that the tours offered by Robben Island are insufficient, but you may want more information than is usually covered in a larger group.

ROBBEN ISLAND
Buy your ferry tickets and board at the Nelson Mandela Gateway, V&A Waterfront
Ferries depart daily at 9am, 10am, 11am, 1pm and 2pm
Advanced booking is recommended
021 413-4200

Personal tours by Indres Naidoo (021 461-5394), or see either www.robben-island.org.za or www.robbenislandtours.com

moving on

LWANDLE MIGRANT LABOUR MUSEUM

The Cape Care Route showcases some of the projects around the Peninsula where people are caring for the environment and one another. Social activist Faizal Gangat is passionate about sustainable development, and a tour through some of the lesser-known parts of Cape Town with him as your guide is truly worthwhile.

Ask him to take you to the Lwandle Migrant Labour Museum which was established to remind us of the legacy of the apartheid policy that exploited the African male workforce. The men were housed in large, impersonal hostels far from their families.

Today the hostels have been converted into family homes, but one has been retained as a reminder of the conditions under which migrant labourers lived. It's a harsh exhibition about a cruel time in our history.

LWANDLE MIGRANT LABOUR MUSEUM
Mondays to Fridays, 9am till 4pm
Saturdays 9pm till 1pm
021 845-6119

Cape Town Tourism (021 426-4260) lists Cape Care Route tour operators, such as Faizal Gangat of Cape Capers Tours 021 448-3117 or 083 358-0193

real café culture

CORNER CAFÉS

KAROO SPRING WATER

Rose Corner CAFE

R CAFE

HOT KOESIESTERS
SUNDAYS

Everyone needs a corner café – a place where the owner greets you like a friend, where you can pick up a late-night loaf of bread, the papers and an urgent pack of cigarettes.

Corner cafés are an increasingly rare phenomenon, being replaced by franchises offering boring uniformity. The Imperial Café on the Foreshore is long gone, as is the Zanzibar Café on Voortrekker Road. But Rose's Corner Café, Lorna Doone and Mr Bawa's place still stand proud, serving the same customers they have for years.

These are shopkeepers in the true sense of the word, offering a sense of community and maintaining old values and traditions.

CORNER CAFÉS

Rose's Corner Café, Rose Street, Bo-Kaap
Lorna Doone, Koeberg Road, Milnerton
Mr Bawa's, Kloof Street, Gardens, or look
around and find your own favourite

camping at the castle

CASTLE OF GOOD HOPE

There is a strong movement afoot to wrest the Castle of Good Hope from its military past. Although it is still home to the Defence Force's Western Province command, the oldest building in Cape Town has recently been the venue of choice for some outrageous happenings.

The Mother City Queer Project had their annual bash here in 2002 and will be holding their tenth anniversary bash there in 2003. The 2002 theme was weddings, and thousands of revellers wearing elaborate dresses, veils, tiaras and a variety of completely camp, over-the-top outfits partied through the night here. The city's forefathers must have been turning in their graves... or perhaps not.

Another stirring event held here was YDESIRE – a celebration of the concept of desire. Video installations were shown in dark corridors, the dolphin pool became a stage for an experimental opera, performance artists invited viewers into their lairs, DJ's played the decks and in every nook and cranny of the old castle people congregated to party, peruse art and revel in the creative freedom of it all.

If you missed these, you can still thrown your own private, never-to-be-forgotten party here. The folks at the very good castle restaurant De Goewerneur will create a menu of traditional South African cuisine for you and your guests and you can hire a venue where you can dance away the ghosts of your past.

CASTLE OF GOOD HOPE
The Grand Parade, CBD
Mondays to Sundays, 9am till 4pm
Free public tours at 11am, 12pm and 2pm daily
Key ceremony, Mondays to Fridays at 10am and 12pm
021 787-1082 or 021 787-1249
www.castleofgoodhope.co.za

De Goewerneur Restaurant
Castle of Good Hope, The Grand Parade, CBD
021 461-4895

starry, starry night

PLANETARIUM AT THE SA MUSEUM

Star-gazing is more than an excuse to snuggle up to someone and whisper sweet nothings. It is a science, one far removed from the 'she's a Virgo, so she's organised' school of thought. A visit to the SA Planetarium will have you looking at the night skies in a far more prosaic and intelligent way.

Armed with a map of the evening sky and a briefing in the general direction of north, south, east and west, you'll leave the lecture a little wiser. It's by no means an easy science, but at the very least you could impress someone with your new-found knowledge the next time you venture outside to 'look at the stars'.

IZIKO MUSEUMS OF CAPE TOWN
PLANETARIUM AT THE SA MUSEUM
25 Queen Victoria Street, top of the Company Gardens, CBD
Mondays to Sundays, 10am till 5pm, lectures are held Mondays
to Fridays at 2pm, Saturdays at 12pm, 1pm and 2.30pm
021 481-3800

inner city blooms

FLOWER SELLERS

The Flower Market just off Adderley Street is a Cape Town landmark. To be a flower seller runs in your blood and it is an occupation passed down from one generation to another.

Each month the vendors shift up one place in a revolving system that provides equal access to the passing trade on Adderley Street. There is a spirit of camaraderie here, and it is the colourful banter between vendors and buyers, as much as the colourful blooms, that gives the market its distinctive character.

The flowers are tightly packed together, richly-coloured roses competing with the purple brilliance of irises, the simple splendour of arum lilies contrasting with the silly shades of carnations. But sadly it is proteas that give the flower sellers a headache. In their distinctive street patois they lament that, with all the choices available, not even tourists buy our strangely beautiful national flower any more. But, whatever your choice, is there anything more evocative than the bright orange of fragile poppies wrapped up in old newsprint?

FLOWER SELLERS
Trafalgar Place, between the Standard Bank building and the Golden Acre, Adderley Street, CBD
Mondays to Saturdays

revisiting
the past

DISTRICT SIX MUSEUM

D istrict Six is a scar on Cape Town's physical and emotional landscape. The apartheid policy of forced removals saw a whole community destroyed here. The remarkable District Six Museum pays tribute to the people and the spirit of the place that stood in the shadow of the mountain.

It is a desperately tragic part of our city's history and the museum commemorates it in an honest, poignant way. The saddest part of the museum, and one that brings the tragedy to life, is the large street map of what District Six looked like before the bulldozers moved in; on it old residents have written their names on the places where they once lived and loved and lost.

DISTRICT SIX MUSEUM
25a Buitenkant Street, CBD
Mondays to Saturdays, 9am till 4pm
021 461-8745
www.districtsix.co.za

EXHAUSTS

pavement
aristocrats

BERGIES

Bergies give colour to our city and psychedelic hues to our language. But the very fact that they exist is an indictment on our society, and how you respond to them, or not, may well be an indictment on you. The city's home-less survive by begging and selling paper waste – you will often see them pushing supermarket trolleys filled with cardboard and piles of paper. According to Francois Verster's brilliant documentary *Pavement Aristocrats*, Bergies are descendants of the seventeenth century Strandlopers who roamed the beaches and mountains.

They're awfully fond of cursing your mother's anatomical parts, and have a repertoire of curses that they use liberally, but treat them with kindness and respect and you will find yourself being given a warm smile and a rough but hilarious piece of street wisdom. One hip couple recounts being silenced while throwing one of their fabulously loud parties by an irate Bergie trying to sleep beneath their win-dow: 'Shut up! Ek probeer slaap hier buite!' Another over-heard a Bergie whose bottle of cheap wine had slipped out of his hands: looking at the wine spreading on the pave-ment, he shook his head dismally. 'Ag naai man, gravity...'

BERGIES

Look out for Marilyn in the Gardens area, and the 'Whistle Man' on the M5 highway.

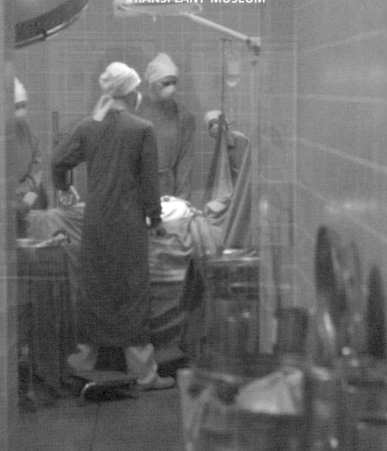

the human touch

TRANSPLANT MUSEUM

S tanding on the top of the roof, the Goddess of Health guards the original Groote Schuur Hospital building. You find yourself wondering if Professor Chris Barnard noted the figure as he left the building on 3 December 1967, having just performed the world's first heart transplant. The transplant museum answers this and other questions.

Built on the site of that first heart transplant, the museum commemorates the historic event that captured the world's imagination and made Chris Barnard a household name. It pays tribute to the courage of the surgeon, the donor Denise Darvall and the recipient Louis Washkansky. A comprehensive display of the newspapers of the day gives you insight into the mood and politics of the time. You can read how the donor's father felt, how Louis Washkansky's courage touched the nation, and how the world reacted to the charmingly good-looking and talented surgeon. A surprising museum, it is far more interesting than one would expect.

TRANSPLANT MUSEUM
1st Floor, Groote Schuur Hospital (Old Building)
Mondays to Fridays, 9am till 2pm
021 404-5232

shalom

SOUTH AFRICAN JEWISH MUSEUM

קק, תקות יש

ER STONE WAS LAID
LENCY the HONOURABLE
R F HELY·HUTCHINSON
VERNOR of the COLONY
19TH SIVAN 5664
2ND JUNE 1904

ועשו לי מקדש ושכנ
ובמקום הזה אתן

After a tight security check at the entrance, you enter the grounds of the SA Jewish Museum, the Cape Town Holocaust Centre, the Great Synagogue and the best café/restaurant on Museum Mile.

The SA Jewish Museum traces the history of the Jewish people, the countries they left behind, how they settled in South Africa and the roles – economic, political and social – that they've played in this country, and celebrates their accomplishments. The Holocaust Centre is a harrowing, but vitally important exhibition, described as 'a place of learning about the disastrous consequences of unchecked race prejudice and inter-group hatred'. A brilliant and moving tribute to the human spirit.

SOUTH AFRICAN JEWISH MUSEUM
88 Hatfield Street, Gardens
Sundays to Thursdays, 10am till 5pm, Fridays, 10am till 2pm
021 465-1546
www.sajewishmuseum.co.za

Cape Town Holocaust Centre
021 462-5553
www.museums.org.za/ctholocaust

Café Riteve
021 465-1594

stern stuff

IRMA STERN MUSEUM

This is one of the loveliest museums in Cape Town and, even if you are a complete art philistine, you will enjoy the voyeuristic element of seeing how a remarkable individual lived her life in the 1920s.

Irma Stern is considered one of South Africa's most important artists. She received greater critical acclaim in Europe than she did in her own country at first, but by the 1940s her work was highly regarded here too.

Stern was not only an artist, but also a collector of African art, and her valuable collection fills her home. But it is her paintings, and the way her art was such an integral part of her home, that make this museum so special. The furniture and doors she painted give a clue as to her true nature. Look out for the Dance of Death cupboard and the one in her diningroom that depicts the Nativity – they tell of a woman unafraid to live her life the way she wanted to.

It's a good place to escape to when you feel the need to be surrounded by beautiful things and to be inspired by a woman strong enough to defy convention.

IRMA STERN MUSEUM
Cecil Road, Rosebank
Tuesdays to Saturdays, 10am till 5pm
021 685-5686

BOULDERS PENGUIN COLONY PG 214

Outdoors

ACTION · ENERGY · NATURE

There's so much more to Cape Town than just lazing about on the beach all day long. That is, of course, the easiest option... but sometimes you just need to head outdoors and build up a little bit of sweat. Going for a hike up the mountain will have you feeling virtuous and paragliding will set your pulse racing, while mountain biking will have you holding onto your seat and a leisurely horse ride will remind you of an even slower pace of life than the one in the Mother City.

back to the beach

MUIZENBERG

Muizenberg is experiencing a revival – with all those fab art deco buildings, it was just waiting to happen. The slumlords seem to be moving out and the bohemians back in. Yes!

Muizenberg has a legendary beach, where the water is warm and the people relaxed and welcoming. It's a great place to escape the city smog; grab the old surfboard and paddle out. If you can't surf, but desperately want to, pop in to Gary's Surf School. A former Western Province surfing coach, Gary Kleinhans can teach anyone to surf, irrespective of age, provided you're keen and can swim. He also rents out boards and wetsuits for those who vaguely remember how to catch a wave and are willing to risk it in front of all the pros.

If surfing isn't your thing, go for a long walk on the beach, or surprise the kids – and yourself – by flying a kite; it may look easy, but it takes some skill, and you'll definitely find yourself working up a sweat.

Afterwards, dry off and cross the railway bridge to the Empire Café – the hippest new eatery in the area. Their banana, honey and bacon omelettes will seduce you, but everything else that's written up on the blackboard looks phenomenal too. The food is eclectic and interesting and, despite the casual vibe, beautifully presented and gorgeously served by the local surfers/waiters.

EXPLORING MUIZENBERG
Gary's Surf School
90 Beach Road, Muizenberg
Mondays to Sundays, 8.30am till 5pm
021 788-9839

EMPIRE CAFÉ
11 York Road, Muizenberg
Tuesdays to Sundays, 7am till 4pm but open
till 9.30pm on Fridays and Saturdays
021 788-1250

coming up roses

CHART FARM

At Chart Farm you get to pick your own roses. It's not nearly as effortless as popping in at Woolies on your way home, but it is a whole lot more fun.

If the weather's nice, head on out to the farm, pick up a pair of scissors and a box and set off for the rows of rosebushes. All are clearly-marked so you can tell your Cora Marie from your Boksberg Fantasia.

Dodging the thorns can be tricky so if you're not in the gardening mood simply buy ready-cut stems and settle down at the Tea Terrace instead. Here, overlooking the vineyards and orchards, you can order proper home-baked cakes and contemplate fruit-picking at a later date.

CHART FARM
Klaassens Road, Wynberg Park
Mondays to Sundays, 9am till 4.30pm
021 761-0434

Tea Terrace
021 762-0067

falling leaves

TOKAI ARBORETUM

Y ou don't need to have a passion for horticulture to appreciate the oldest tree park in South Africa. A leisurely walk through the falling leaves is all that's required to make a trip to the Tokai Arboretum worth your while. The smallest of leaves will catch the sunlight, the wind will rustle in the treetops and the forest sounds will calm you.

Should you need refreshments, there is a tearoom that serves homemade cakes and one or two specials of the day. It's a rather dreary-looking place, so order your food and eat it outside beneath the trees.

You may want to go horse riding or mountain biking (permits available at the gate), hiking or even mushroom-picking if that's your thing, but it really is okay just to look at the light filtering through the trees.

TOKAI ARBORETUM
M3 to Muizenberg, take the Tokai/Retreat turnoff, right into Tokai Road and left on reaching Tokai Manor House
Mondays to Sundays, during daylight hours
021 712-7471

who let the
dogs out?

ADAM JAMES — PROFESSIONAL DOG WALKER

With his pack of dogs, Adam is a familiar sight in Tamboerskloof and Gardens. Single-handedly, he manages to walk up to sixteen dogs at a time. Dressed in a bright yellow sweatshirt and wind-breaker, he is the alpha-male who seems to control the pack effortlessly.

Adam James enjoys the company of his canine friends. 'I'm not good at communicating with people, but I am good at communicating with dogs,' he has said. Which makes me wonder, do we have our very own Dog Whisperer in the City Bowl?

The canines come from all walks of life; Labradors, huskies, spaniels, Jack Russells and some of mixed descent. They have just two things in common: they like the company of other dogs and they adore Adam who liberates them from monotonous days in their owners' backyards. He collects them from their homes early in the morning and they set off for De Waal Park to play in a sociable environment where no fighting is permitted.

There can be no doubt who top dog in the park is – all it takes is just one short bark from Adam and the dogs obey. Playfulness is rewarded by a cuddle and a wet-nose kiss. Looking on, you're unsure who's enjoying themselves more – man or mutt.

For onlookers though, it's their route to the park and back that's the fun bit, Adam's skilful manoeuvring of his pack of dogs is an impressive sight.

Try catching up with them and seeing up-close how this remarkable man deals with his charges. And it may also spur you to action – shouldn't *your* dog be out walking?

**ADAM JAMES –
PROFESSIONAL
DOG WALKER**
Gardens area
Catch him if you can!
083 413-7879

get high

TANDEM PARAGLIDING WITH PARA-PAX

Not everyone wants to invest time and money in learning how to paraglide, but that doesn't stop us from wondering what it feels like to fly. Stef from Para-Pax gives all those who wish to explore the skies and soar the mountain tops, but don't want to go it alone, the opportunity to fly with an expert.

On offer is a professional outfit with an oversized, specially-designed tandem glider and two harnesses that will guarantee you the most amazing flight. Tandem Paragliding is an incredible way to feel the exhilaration of 'free-flight' in safe and experienced hands. You get to be in front, which means you have an uninterrupted view of the ocean, mountain and city beneath you as you take off from Lion's Head or Signal Hill.

It's not a frightening thrill, just a great rush.

TANDEM PARAGLIDING WITH PARA-PAX
By appointment only, through the week and weather permitting
Stef on 082 881-4724
www.parapax.com

smartly
dressed birds

BOULDERS PENGUIN COLONY

No matter how many times you see these birds, the novelty doesn't wear off. African penguins are a vulnerable species, but they have managed to find a haven on one of the prettiest beaches in the Cape Peninsula.

In 1982 Boulders Beach was home to two breeding penguin pairs. Today, well over three thousand birds call the beach home. Watching them go about their daily business, scrambling over vegetation and caring for their fluffy grey babies will fill you with a strong desire to do the same – so don't visit if your own nesting instinct is in overdrive and your biological clock is ticking!

The Cape Peninsula National Park charges a R10 entrance fee, which allows you access to the small, protected swimming beach as well as the walkways that take you to within a few metres of the birds. Look out for Van the Penguin Man, the local penguin expert.

With their distinctive tuxedo colouring and comical waddle, the birds provide endless amusement. They cock their heads sideways as if puzzled by all the attention and then get on with their idyllic lives.

BOULDERS PENGUIN COLONY
Boulders Beach (between Simon's Town and Cape Point)
Mondays to Sundays, 8am till 5pm
021 786-2329

down the drain

180° ADVENTURES – STORMWATER CANALS

While Cape Town may not have Tube transport, we do have an underground network of walkways. This is not, of course, the answer to the city's transport problems, nor is it accessible to everyone. But it is worth exploring.

Part of the network dates back to 1652, Jan van Riebeeck's era, and the underground canals are large enough for people to walk through – during the dry season, obviously. Xavier Scheepers is the man who will expose you to the darker side of Cape Town city life. As a former engineer, it's only natural that he would have found out more about the subterranean water system, and arranged permission for his company, 180° Adventures, to use it. If you're squeamish and worried about rats and other undesirables, don't be. Evidently the crawlier creatures know that these are stormwater drains, and that they will be flushed out whenever it rains. So the canals are safe (in the dry season), clean and very, very interesting.

It's about an hour-long, rather spooky walk in the dark, with torches. But you're in safe hands as Xavier is a Camel man; yup, the real thing. (He won the Camel Trophy International event in Tonga in 2000.) He is also extremely knowledgeable about the history of the

drains, and there's something oddly special about being underneath the city. The world above gets on with its daily existence, completely unaware of the historic, undercover perspective on city life being discovered by a select few.

Although the canals flow all the way to the sea, Xavier will have you popping up through a manhole set in the manicured lawn of the Castle.

180° ADVENTURES – EXPLORING THE CITY'S STORMWATER DRAINS
By appointment only
021 712-6960
www.180.co.za

fly by night

BASE 4 HELICOPTER FLIP

Imagine seeing the Mother City from the air, as you glide through the night skies over blankets of fairy-lights, tracing the orange glow of highways and seeing Table Mountain from a new perspective...

BASE 4 Helicopters are the only outfit equipped to offer helicopter trips around the peninsula at night – and their moonlit flights shed an entirely new light on the city's neon-soaked landmarks.

The flips last thirty minutes each, and the four-seater helicopter is the perfect vehicle in which to explore the city in an intriguing new way.

BASE 4 HELICOPTER FLIP
Depart Cape Town International Airport
By appointment only, through the week and weather permitting
021 934-4405

sail away

GOOD HOPE SAILING ACADEMY

If the yachting life appeals to you, or your current situation is such that you'd like to pack it all in and park off on a deserted island somewhere sunny and stress-free, then you need to give the Good Hope Sailing Academy a call.

Based at Royal Cape Yacht Club in the Cape Town harbour (very good membership card to have – excellent clubhouse!), this academy can teach you all you need to know in order to embark on some thrilling exercise or a lifelong dream. They offer the Competent Crew course for beginners where you'll learn the basics of sailing. On completion you'll be able to take on the responsibility of Watch Master when the skipper is off watch.

Provided the seasickness doesn't mess up your ambitions, you'll soon be joining the crews on the lively Wednesday evening club races at RCYC and working on that tan.

GOOD HOPE SAILING ACADEMY
Royal Cape Yacht Club, Cape Town Harbour
021 426-1153

get nekkid!

SANDY BAY – NUDIST BEACH

F or years, Sandy Bay has been
has been a haven for nudists.
A beautiful piece of coastline, it's
where you can get it all off and let
it all hang out.

The water is cold and there aren't
any facilities, so bring along whatever
you need. But it is still one of the
best-loved spots on the Cape coast,
with shrubs and boulders offering
privacy for the more modest visitor.

Do remember the sunscreen...
for obvious reasons.

SANDY BAY – NUDIST BEACH

Leave your car in the Llandudno car park.
From there it's an easy 25-minute walk
through the fynbos and across some rocks
Anytime

an urban oasis

OUDE MOLEN FARM VILLAGE

The first fresh produce farm in the old Cape Colony, Oude Molen is now the last remaining farm in the city. Until six years ago it made up part of Valkenberg mental hospital, but today it is a micro-enterprise village consisting of artists' studios, woodworkers' workshops, a vegetarian restaurant and meditation centre.

The village aims to demonstrate how under-utilised public assets can be used creatively to launch business and employment opportunities – which all sounds rather heavy-going, but it's not. Healthy types will love the organic produce, and everyone will find inspiration at the studios. If you're comfortable in the saddle, Howard Krut has his stables on the farm and will take you on some unusual and worthwhile horse trails.

OUDE MOLEN FARM VILLAGE
Oude Molen Farm, Alexandra Road, Pinelands
For horse riding call Howard Krut on 021 448-6419

take a hike

WALK WITH MIKE LUNDY

Mike Lundy has written numerous books and hundreds of newspaper columns about hiking, particularly hiking on Table Mountain. He's a household name – even among those who would never dream of owning a pair of hiking boots. In fact, a survey found that eighty-six percent of his readers never set foot on the mountain, nor did they have any intention of doing so. If he has that kind of response from a bunch of couch potatoes, imagine what a hike with him as your guide would be like!

His expertise doesn't come cheap, so it's best to get a group of people together and split the cost, but it will be well worth it. Mike Lundy is passionate about the mountain, its vegetation, animals and birdlife.

WALK WITH MIKE LUNDY
021 790-2048
www.hikecapetown.co.za
Read Mike's guide, *Best Walks in the Cape Peninsula*
Struik Publishers – R85.95

a bunch of balls

THE RIVER CLUB GOLF DRIVING RANGE

If you're an aspirant Ernie Els, or just tired of missing out on all those corporate golf days, the River Club Golf Driving Range is where you can get a few lessons, hit a few balls, and practise without the fear of embarrassing yourself on the golf course.

There also happens to be a good bistro and bar in the old building, so after a hard day at work, you can perfect your golf swing *and* take him out for dinner! Or gather some friends, beat the hell out a few white balls and then drown your sorrows with a few cold ones.

THE RIVER CLUB GOLF DRIVING RANGE
Corner of Liesbeek Parkway and Observatory Road, Observatory
Mondays to Sundays, 8.30am till 9pm
021 447-3757